Counseling for Liberation

Charlotte Holt Clinebell

Fortress Press Philadelphia

Creative Pastoral Care and Counseling Series
Editor: Howard J. Clinebell, Jr.
Associate Editor: Howard W. Stone

The Care and Counseling of Youth in the Church by Paul B. Irwin

Growth Counseling for Marriage Enrichment: Pre-Marriage and the Early Years by Howard J. Clinebell, Jr.

Crisis Counseling by Howard W. Stone

Pastoral Care and Counseling in Grief and Separation by Wayne E. Oates

Counseling for Liberation by Charlotte Holt Clinebell

Library of Congress Catalog Card Number 75–36447

ISBN 0–8006–0555–1

5402–C76   Printed in U.S.A.   1–555

...a part of me is missing

Where is "me"
a part of me is missing
aborted—still born—
since that Garden time

yet, without plan or warning
ever and ever again moving
deep within my body
and soul
a person   "image of God"
WOMAN
comes gasping, grasping
for the breath of life
struggling to be born
and live—free

pushed back, covered over by
myriad words—intoned word
you are not man
you are woman
created for a man's pleasure
and comfort
created to bear man-child
to rule you
created to bear woman-child
to be subject to man-child

Man-child, oh man-child
my father, husband, brothers, sons
do you feel a deep stirring,
rebellion
at the intoned word for you?
*You are man, be big
be strong, powerful
never surrender: succeed
let no tears break through
be mind, not heart
heart is for the weak
be arrogant—aggressive*

CRY, CRY BELOVED IMAGE
Who calls us both?

—Anne McGrew Bennett,
Women in a Strange Land

Contents

Series Foreword

Let me share with you some of the hopes that are in the minds of those of us who helped to develop this series—hopes that relate directly to you as the reader. It is our desire and expectation that these books will be of help to you in developing better working tools as a minister-counselor. We hope that they will do this by encouraging your own creativity in developing more effective methods and programs for helping people live life more fully. It is our intention in this series to affirm the many things you have going for you as a minister in helping troubled persons—the many assets and resources from your religious heritage, your role as the leader of a congregation, and your unique relationship to individuals and families throughout the life cycle. We hope to help you reaffirm *the power of the pastoral* by the use of fresh models and methods in your ministry.

The aim of the series is not to be comprehensive with respect to topics but rather to bring innovative approaches to some major types of counseling. Although the books are practice-oriented, they also provide a solid foundation of theological and psychological insights. They are written primarily for ministers (and those preparing for the ministry) but we hope that they will also prove useful to other counselors who are interested in the crucial role of spiritual and value issues in all helping relationships. In addition we hope that the series will be useful in seminary courses, clergy support groups, continuing education workshops, and lay befriender training.

This is a period of rich new developments in counseling and psychotherapy. The time is ripe for a flowering of creative methods and insights in pastoral care and counseling. Our expectation is that this series will stimulate grass roots creativity as innovative methods and programs come alive for you. Some of the major thrusts that will be discussed in this series include a new awareness of the unique contributions of the theologically trained counselor, the liberating power of the human potentials orientation, an appreciation of the pastoral care function of the ministering congregation, the importance of humanizing systems and institutions as well as close relationships, the importance of pastoral *care* (and not just counseling), the many opportunities for caring ministries throughout the life cycle, the deep changes in male-female relationships, and the new psychotherapies such as Gestalt therapy, transactional analysis, educative counseling, and crisis methods. Our hope is that this series will enhance your resources for your ministry to persons by opening doorways to understanding of these creative thrusts in pastoral care and counseling.

This volume by Charlotte Holt Clinebell deals with what is probably the most profound interpersonal revolution of our times. It is a revolution which is gradually changing the way each half of the human family is treating the other half. The book explores implications of the changing identities of women and men for pastoral care and counseling. It will be useful both to pastors and to lay leaders who are committed to helping churches become more effective centers of human liberation by eliminating the blight of sexism.

This book reflects the author's personal experiences in the church as well as her professional experience as a psychotherapist and a marriage, family, and child counselor. Charlotte is a dedicated participant in the women's liberation movement and counsels with many women, men, and couples who are feeling the shaking impact of changing roles.

On a more personal level, I happen to know that she also works at liberating her intimate relationships. As an individual she knows the excitement of discovering new dimensions of herself and developing a new, nonderivative identity. She knows what it is like to struggle toward a more liberated marriage with a husband who blends openness and resistance to change with frustrating ambivalence. I owe the author of this volume a profound debt for helping me, through the contagion of her own liberation, gradually to become aware of my need for liberation from much of my male programming.

This book is on the growing edge of pastoral counseling. It offers a variety of practical methods for integrating counseling and consciousness raising. It confronts those of us us who are male ministers and counselors with the urgent necessity to get our own consciousness raised. Only thus can we become better facilitators of human liberation.

The future viability of pastoral care and counseling depends, to a considerable extent, on our response to the issues raised by this book. The growth possibilities for persons, around these issues, are enormous. I predict that this book will ruffle some feathers, elevate some eye-brows, and, more importantly, raise consciousness and motivate action to liberate the church and the counselor, as well as the recipients of counseling.

HOWARD J. CLINEBELL, JR.

Introduction:
Slow Motion Earthquake

> We do not yet talk about how much we all are interdependent and need to relate to an equal, how challenging and beneficial that process can be, how often this need is thwarted, how little practice we get in it, and how much of our life is spent at the much more primitive level of learning how to be either one-up or one-down.*   —Jean Baker Miller

The rumble of an approaching earthquake can be heard in the distance. As the ground shakes, unstable structures come crashing down. Damage is done; people are hurt. The landscape is rearranged. Sometimes new beauty arises from the destruction. A new mountain may begin to appear or a waterfall start its flow; a beautiful new city may rise from the rubble of the old one.

The rumbling upheaval in relationships between the sexes is much like a slow-motion earthquake. The rumbling is getting much louder and the motion is accelerating. Already, old "truths" are threatened. Our most cherished beliefs about women and men and how they should relate to each other are being challenged and are crumbling around us. Already we feel and hear the rumble in our homes and schools, our churches and offices, even—perhaps especially—in our bedrooms. Much of our civilization is built upon a system of dominance-submission between the sexes. When the most basic relationship begins to change, everything else must change as well. It is difficult to predict what sort of society will emerge as we struggle toward more egalitarian relationships.

* For this and all other notes in this book, see the Notes section beginning on p. 81.

Will we simply build something new on the same old fault?   Or will the new structures be stronger, more beautiful, more enduring, more fully humanizing for both women and men?

The current revolution in roles has two basic thrusts—to bring full equality of opportunity and treatment for women and men, and to end the hierarchical system which keeps some people on the bottom so others can be on the top.   If these two things happen—and they are surely interdependent—a new and benevolent order of civilization may emerge in which every individual can lead a satisfying life.   The very suggestion of such an outcome has an idealistic ring.   But do we not inherit a faith which affirms the abundant life for *all*, not just for some?   We know already that it is possible to bring together our most impossible dreams and our expertise in order to land ourselves on the moon.   Would not a similar commitment allow us to realize the Arcadian vision of a human civilization which makes the fullness of life possible for everyone?

The church, like all other institutions of our society, has for 2000 years built its house of relationships between the sexes on a shaky foundation.   The result has been equally dehumanizing, though in different ways, for both women and men. There are some signs of change, but there is still great resistance in the churches (and in the counseling professions) to a new view of human wholeness which would include women as well as men.   The reluctance of many churches and church bodies to accept ordination of women is a case in point. Women ministers are still rejected by many laypersons of both sexes.   Often they are assigned to low paying and low status jobs.   There continues to be a dearth of women in pastoral counseling.   Sexism as an ethical issue is largely ignored by the church and by its related bodies.

The "uniqueness" of pastoral counseling and of the minister as counselor has been taken to mean that these disciplines speak with an especially liberating power because of their great religious and biblical heritage.   But to fully half the human race—women—the Judeo-Christian tradition has all too often not been liberating.   "Perhaps the greatest pain women bear from the church is the verbal offer of liberation while being pushed to the periphery of the church's life and ministry."* It is time that "the truth that makes us free" be revived and reinterpreted to include all persons. It is time to raise new questions about what it is to be "human" as well as "religious" in the church, a setting which has almost always equated "human" with "male," and "male" with power and dominance, and has valued women chiefly as virgins, wives, mothers, servants or occasionally as saints.

Like the rest of society, the church is feeling the shaking of its foundations as women challenge their traditional roles with increasing vehemence. Change means pain, and the church is feeling that pain, as are the women and men who *are* the church. The pain for me as a woman who has grown up in the church is my awareness that pastoral counselors, ministers, and laypersons are all too often of a closed mind, deaf to the issue of sexism in the church. I often feel that the church may be the *least* hopeful place to put my time and energies. Will anyone listen? Will anyone hear? As I struggle to write this book, my pain often expresses itself in anger. I hope that you who read will not take my anger personally, but will use it to get in touch with your own. Often the awareness of anger at a repressive system is itself enough to stimulate change.

It has also been my experience in speaking and writing that some people *do* listen and some *do* hear and respond. This book is written out of my hope that "their number is increasing." And it isn't just women who are hearing; men are responding too. I feel a warm glow and a sense of affirmation when I learn of churches which are eliminating sexist language from their worship services and liturgy, of ministers who are studying and preaching about feminist theology and the Mother-Father God, of consciousness-raising groups and task forces on sexism in the church.

All good counseling is consciousness raising, that is, helping a client or counselee or parishioner to discover and nurture her or his full and unique humanness. Any theory or method of counseling is ethical and effective in nurturing individual and collective wholeness if it views every individual first as a person, rather than first as a woman or a man. We have for centuries made the mistake of equating *femaleness* and *maleness,* which are biological terms, with *femininity* and *masculinity* which are cultural terms. What the upheaval in changing roles and identities is making clear is that the feelings and behaviors traditionally labeled either "feminine" or "masculine" are not characteristic of either sex alone but are human responses. Assertiveness, independence, passivity, and gentleness are all part of being human, whether female or male. In the pages that follow, therefore, the two words *feminine* and *masculine* will appear in quotation marks in recognition of the limitations of our language and culture. It is not that either set of traits, those associated with "feminine" or those associated with "masculine," is bad—both are good. It is simply that we have divided them up so rigidly between the sexes. A new experience of wholeness for both women and men can result from the conjoining of the "masculine" and the "feminine" in which all human powers are quickened.

This book, then, is not mainly about counseling theory and technique. It is instead an attempt to describe the important connection between good counseling and consciousness raising. Some techniques for use in that effort are included. It is my increasing conviction that a large percentage of the psychological-spiritual problems people bring to counseling result from the tight boxes our culture has forced us into as women and men. This book is about the pain people are feeling because of these confining boxes *and* because many are now trying to get out of them. The message of the book can be stated in one sentence: As ministers and counselors it is up to us to do whatever we can to get out of our own boxes, while at the same time trying to help other people get out of theirs.

We need to talk to each other; we need to try to hear and understand each other's anger and pain, and not be put off by it. Our goal is not to end the relationship between the sexes, but to improve and enhance it. Through its counseling and caring ministries the church can be a major agency for change

—for rebuilding on a strong foundation the relationship between women and men. Not long ago, at a communion service in which couples fed each other the elements, a young man suggested that we could say as we served the wine to each other, "This is the cup of the new relationship." It is my belief that as we discover that new relationship we will find new and more effective ways to assure life in all its fullness for every human being.

1. The Issues in a Fishbowl

Also, the idea that, as women become more secure, men become more insecure, and vice versa, makes one wonder. Is it really true that we are on a teetertotter and that only one sex can be secure at a time?*   —Mabel Blake Cohen

Consciousness Raising, Fishbowl Style

Seven women sat on the floor in a circle, talking with one another. Surrounding them in a larger circle sat seven men listening intently. Around the room, eyes and ears concentrated on the inner circles, perhaps forty more people were gathered. From time to time as the women spoke, an exclamation, a gasp, a sigh, an oath could be heard from outside the inner circle. An observer, glancing about the room, could see heads shaking, tears welling up in some eyes, an angry expression here, a delighted one there.

CAROL: Sometimes I think things are getting better for women. But then something happens. A couple of weeks ago we were in a restaurant with friends. I noticed a large bronze plaque on the wall at the other end of the room. It said:

Four Things a Woman Should Know

How to look like a girl
How to act like a lady
How to work like a horse
How to think like a man

Most of the men in our party thought the plaque hilariously funny. One of the women said she just ignored things like that. The waitress said, "That's the way it *is* around here!"

6

The cashier said she didn't like it but she didn't know what to do about it. I was so angry, it ruined my whole evening!

ANN: But what made you so angry? You hear silly things like that all the time. It doesn't really mean anything.

MOLLY: Oh, yes it does! It's a real put-down, the sort of thing that makes something go *click* inside. You know, when all of a sudden it strikes you that you're in a box and someone is trying to keep you there, and you say to yourself. "Oh, no you don't!" It happened to me when my six-year-old son came home from school saying he was planning to be governor some day. I said I thought that was just great, I'd often thought of running for office myself. He said, "Oh mom, you can't do that. You're a woman." *Click!* Here I thought I was such a liberated mother raising liberated children. That blew my mind. The school has more influence than I do!

ANN: But why would you want to be governor anyway?

ALICE: Ann, I want to be free to do anything I'm capable of doing. I don't want to be told it's wrong for a woman, or that I'm "unfeminine" when I do something aggressive or strong.

CAROL: What makes me mad is being treated like an appendage to my husband. I like being Carol, not Mrs. Joe Smith. If I must have a title then I prefer Ms. It makes me furious when I see all those "Mrs. Joe So-and-Sos" listed in the church bulletin. Haven't they got names of their own? Aren't they people too, even though they have husbands?

MARY: I agree with all this, but, it's scary! What do you do when you realize after ten years of marriage and two kids that either you have to leave or you die inside? I kept hoping that my husband would see the reasonableness of my wanting things different. He didn't. He wanted the woman he married—the straight housewife-mother. So now I'm a divorcée. In spite of that *awful* word, I'm a lot freer and happier person. But I'd still like to know if it's possible to make it with a man and remain a human being.

CAROL: Well, I think it's possible, but it isn't easy. And I think a man has to be willing to change too, and to see women in a different light, and to try to understand our anger. Joe thought that sign in the restaurant was funny at first, but when he saw how angry I was, he gave it some thought. The hardest thing for him, I think, is that since I've gone to work I'm not as available as cook, laundress, and mother. He has to share those chores. I guess I'll feel we've arrived when he thinks of those things as truly *his* responsibility too and not just that he's helping *me* out.

MARY: I can't even imagine it. I'm afraid even to think about marriage again—it feels like prison to me.

ELAINE: One of you said something about the church. That's been one of the hardest struggles for me since I got my consciousness raised. And if you think that isn't a problem when you're married to a minister! I can hardly bring myself even to attend church any more, partly because of the all-male language and symbolism of the services, partly because women are expected to stay in the kitchen and the church school classroom and the pew, and partly because even the Bible seems to make women inferior.

CAROL: Well, I just don't go to church anymore. But then, I'm not a minister's wife. I do miss it though. I keep hoping the church will change.

ANN: I can't understand what all of you are saying! It sounds like you all think it's not good or satisfying to be a housewife. Can't you be liberated, whatever that means, and still enjoy homemaking as a career? I *enjoy* being a wife and mother. I *like* being home with my kids and being there when my husband come home at night. I *like* working at church suppers. And I resent being told I'm not liberated because I do. A woman who is happy being a wife and mother and homemaker shouldn't be made to feel less respected and worthwhile than a woman who has a job or career. Most of us who are content with home and family have happier marriages!

MOLLY: Well, that may be true for you Ann, but when I got

married I wasn't aware there *were* any other options. Now I'm struggling to add other dimensions, which doesn't mean I don't like my husband or my marriage. Ann, you said something about a woman being happy as a wife and mother and homemaker. Well, of course she *can* be! But if that's worthwhile and respectable for women then it ought to be worthwhile and respectable for men too. Just try changing that sentence of yours to say "man": "A man who is happy being a husband and father and homemaker should be respected . . ." How does that grab you?

ANN: But that's different . . .

LAURA: You know I've been sitting here listening to all of you talk and getting more and more churned up inside . . . (Here a hushed silence fell over the room as Laura struggled with her tears.) This is one reason I haven't talked up to now—I knew I'd get emotional about it . . . You know, this is the first time I've been in a group with other women who feel the way I do. I've felt so alone . . . Of course, I've read about these things, and it's all over the papers, but mostly the media put the whole thing down. When I have mentioned some of my feelings I've been labeled a "crazy women's libber." I thought there must be something wrong with me, that I feel this way. I like my husband and my children and some of the things I do, but right now I *hate* my life! I'm angry—that's the first time I've admitted that to myself, much less to anyone else. I'm tired of letting myself be used and abused by my family—and they don't even know what's wrong. I'm not sure I do either. I'm tired of feeling inhibited and limited and intimidated and helpless. And I suppose this discussion today really gets to me because I suddenly feel less alone, like maybe my anger isn't all my fault. It's frightening too . . . where I live I'm so alone . . . What am I going to do about it all? . . .

After forty-five minutes of discussion among the seven women of the inner circle, they were asked to change places with the seven men who had been sitting around them listening and watching. The seven men now in the inner circle were asked to talk with each other about their own reactions to what they had heard the women saying:

JERRY: Well, I must say this has all been a shock to me. Most of what I hear about women's lib sounds pretty far out—like a bunch of women who couldn't make it airing their complaints. But today it sounded different. I hadn't really realized that women are hurting so much. I suppose it makes me feel a little guilty.

BILL: I wonder if they really are hurting or if they're just whining. I'm glad my wife isn't here today. She hasn't got such a bad life. I make a good living; she doesn't have to work. I wouldn't want her to. The kids aren't that much trouble and she has all the household appliances money can buy. She doesn't have to worry about earning a living. I can't see what any of these women are complaining about.

JOE: Well, Bill, just wait till your wife gets her consciousness raised. That poem Carol read—sure I laughed like all the others—it seemed funny and not very serious. And of course, Carol was madder at me than at anybody else for laughing. But if I'm honest with myself, I have to admit that I do tend to see a woman first as a sex object—I look her up and down, and if she doesn't appeal I classify her as mannish, or domineering, or plain, or old. I certainly don't look at her as an intelligent or competent human being. Not that I'm very proud of that. I'm just now beginning to try to see women as persons. And incidentally, I do see the housework as my responsibility too. I just don't like it and I avoid it if I can! (Laughter)

JIM: I agree with Bill. I think they *are* just a bunch of "crazy women's libbers." I didn't happen to know any of these particular women before, and I'm sure that individually they're very sweet gals; but together they're a bunch of witches. Ann is the only one who makes sense. And all this business about the church! Women are taking over there too. We had a woman minister at our church on

Sunday. It's against everything in the Bible. And worrying about the language! It's ridiculous. Next thing you know, God will be a she!

BEN: I don't feel as strongly about it as you do, Jim. But I do wonder what will happen to all the values we've always believed in. With so many women getting out of the home we're already seeing increased family breakdown and divorce and more kids on drugs and the crime rate rising. Motherhood is the greatest and most important job there is and it's a woman's natural calling. Where will we be if women give it up?

AL: I believe in motherhood too, but I also believe in fatherhood. And I think our experience, Elaine's and mine, has been that as she has put less emphasis on her motherhood role, and more on herself as a person, she's been a better mother . . . and I'm a better father. I spend more time with the children and enjoy them more. When Elaine first started talking about shared parenting and shared homemaking I thought she was crazy. Now I don't think so. It's let me out of my box too.

MICHAEL: I've been sitting here wishing that Judith were here. I'd give anything if she would get interested in something besides me and the kids and the church. I don't mean getting a job, unless she wants one. . . . But I'd like to be able to share ideas with her, and do more stimulating things together and not have our lives always revolving around the kids. What's it going to be like for us when the kids are grown? Maybe I'm also feeling heavy about the burden a breadwinning father and husband has to carry. Sometimes I think, what if I fail? Maybe I'm beginning to wonder about the whole "be a man" philosophy. If Judith were here today maybe we could open up some of these areas.

The seven women and men in the two inner circles were now requested to join each other in one circle, where they immediately began talking all at once and very excitedly to each other while the larger group around the room continued to listen. Some of the women were very angry:

MOLLY: Some of you guys who are talking about motherhood and a woman's natural calling and very sweet gals and all that really make me furious. I don't know whether to laugh or to ignore you, or to fight back. I suppose for myself I've sort of decided that I have to do what is right for me, even if a lot of people don't like it. It seems to me that it ought to be possible for a woman to be married and be a parent and do other things too, just as a man can.

ELAINE: One of you, I think it was Jim, said something about women taking over. Is that what's worrying you? Do you really think we want to take over or that we could? Is it because you're *afraid* of us that you want to keep us in our places? (She sounded incredulous.)

JOE: Well, I confess that when Carol started changing, and wanted an equal say in our decisions, and wanted to have her life considered as important as mine, I did think maybe she wanted to be the boss. I also thought I might lose her! Would she really want to stay with me if she wasn't dependent on me?

JIM: I'm not afraid of women. I just think they ought to do what they were meant to do and stop trying to take over. I get the feeling they want to be on top and put men on the bottom.

CAROL: That's not what I'm talking about at all. I don't want to take over. I just want an equal partnership and the same opportunity to use all of myself in whatever ways are OK for me. When I get angry, it doesn't mean I want to take over or that I want to leave.

ALICE: I felt really hurt when Bill said he thought we were all just whining—that we really don't feel angry and hurt. That pushes me away almost more than the "stay in your place" put-down. It's the sort of thing that makes me feel, well, maybe I *do* have to get along without men if they're not even going to take me seriously. When what I *really* want is just to be *friends*. Aren't there any men who want that too?

AL: I think that's what some of us have been trying to say, if you'd only listen! There *are* men who do. It's been a real struggle for me to change, especially when Elaine starts raising questions about the church. I *am* a minister after all. But women have been treated as second-class, in the church as well as everywhere else, including our marriage. I want that to change—I want to be friends with women, and especially Elaine.

LAURA: Well, Al, all I have to say is that I wish our pastor felt the way you do. I know some ministers are different, but when I went to see our minister he told me I had no real reason to be discontent, because I had everything a woman could possibly want—a good husband, a home, nice children; he said I ought to pray about it and get right with God.

MARY: Trust in God, she will provide! (laughter) I had a different experience when I went to our minister for marriage counseling before our divorce. He could see the problem and really tried to help me be patient and encourage my ex-husband to accept some changes. It wasn't the minister's fault that we parted. But after my divorce I felt ignored by the church. It seems that everywhere I go there's not much place for singles; only couples are acceptable. Of course single men are always in demand. But a single woman is a liability and a failure. In spite of that, I've discovered that it *is* possible to be happy and single—now that I feel good about myself. Also I'm not that "very sweet gal" that Jim describes! I like my independence and freedom and I'll keep right on fighting for it.

The discussion among the fourteen women and men in the inner circle continued intensely for some time. Then the group was asked to open the discussion to the larger audience sitting around the room, many of whom were having trouble keeping quiet any longer.

Several women felt with Laura—and it was a revelation to them to discover that they were not alone in their feelings.

One woman felt a closer kinship with Ann; she said, "Why do we have to get so angry with each other? It isn't right. That's the trouble with this women's lib thing. It stirs up a lot of problems that otherwise wouldn't be there." That comment made others angry; one person expressed her feeling that the words *lib* and *libber* are put-downs—The women's liberation movement is a serious thing and shouldn't be referred to lightly or flippantly.

One man in the audience said he was impressed with how the seven women in the inner circle got immediately to their feelings and related at a deep level, whereas the seven men were mostly head-tripping. Another man remarked that he thought that wasn't true of this particular group but that in general it *is* difficult for men to express their feelings; they weren't brought up that way, they're supposed to be rational and not have feelings. A woman in the audience said she heard the men expressing lots of feelings but some of them copping out on their own responsibilities. She suggested directly to Michael that he take the risk of sharing his feelings with Judith instead of waiting for other people to raise her consciousness: How would she know what he wanted if he didn't tell her?

This session of a consciousness raising group, fishbowl style, took place at a weekend Conference on Human Liberation. The session, originally scheduled to run for two hours, actually went on for three. People became so deeply involved that they didn't even notice they were missing lunch. The intensity of such an experience is not unusual. It is happening with increasing frequency as the consciousness raising style of the women's movement is spreading to mixed groups and to men's groups as well. As women have begun to get in touch with their feelings about being women in our society and as men begin to notice changes in the women they know best, and in the collective consciousness of women, relationships between women and men are beginning to change dramatically. The excitement and chaos, fear and anticipation, that this rising movement brings with it is being felt at every level of our individual and collective lives.

Consciousness raising, then, is simply the bringing into conscious awareness of those influences which cause us to feel and behave as we do. Without such awareness, we cannot have conscious choice about the way we live. Consciousness raising can happen in any area. All of us these days are having our consciousness raised, for example, about the ways in which we are polluting our environment and destroying our natural resources. Once we become aware of what is happening we have some power to change things if we wish to.

Awareness of the Issues

The fishbowl consciousness raising group described above was focusing on the rapidly changing relationships between the sexes. Many important concerns of both women and men were raised in that session. Some of the issues for the women were:

1. Anger at the many subtle and "humorous" put-downs of women.

2. The desire to be involved in education, employment and government as well as the home.

3. The desire to be free to feel and to act on feelings formerly considered only the province of men.

4. Wanting the role of mother and homemaker valued in a new way.

5. Wanting the church to take a fairer attitude toward women.

6. Awareness of the loneliness of being single in a couple-oriented society.

7. The need for a language which includes women.

8. The need for counselors and ministers who are open to the new identities of women.

9. The desire for a new kind of relationship with men.

For men, some of the issues raised were:

1. The importance of emphasizing that male boxes too are tight.

2. Awareness of heavy and often unfair financial burdens.

3. Awareness of not feeling free to be tender and vulnerable.

4. The fear that women want to take over.

5. The fear of being abandoned by women who no longer need men.

6. A concern for what will happen to children and the family.

7. The question of feeling OK when no longer in a one-up position.

8. Guilt over the realization that women are hurting so much.

9. The possibility of some gains in a new kind of relationship with women.

These issues and the many others raised by the changing relationships between the sexes are both personal and social and have tremendous significance for the church. Many of the problems stirred up by the fact of changing roles are bringing individuals, couples, and families for counseling. These issues and problems are causing many people to insist on a different response from the church. Both women and men need, and are asking for, the kind of counseling and consciousness raising which will help them challenge old stereotypes and liberate more fully their spiritual, mental, emotional, and physical potential. The following chapters will look at the role that ministers and counselors can have in facilitating the fullest kind of personal growth in themselves and others.

Inevitably this book leans more heavily on the needs of women. There are two reasons for that. (1) The book is written by a woman, and therefore from a woman's point of view. I find it hard to know how men feel or to believe that they hurt as much as women do. (2) Generally speaking, it is the women who are angry today and asking for change; it is therefore through women that change must begin to come. But men need consciousness raising and liberating too; their anger, while initially a response to the changes women are seeking, often evolves to an awareness of the way sex role stereotyping has limited them too. In the long run, no one is free unless everyone is free. This book, therefore, in spite of its emphasis on women's needs, is a book about human liberation.

2. The Liberated Counselor

Although the women are successfully feminine, as the culture defines it, they are limited if not infantile in their growth in the intellectual, social, and mastery aspects of living. The men are successful masculine types but are limited as human beings by rigidity, fear of and avoidance of emotion, and inability to participate in comfortable intimate relationships.*

—Mabel Blake Cohen

The Counselor's View of Women

In thinking about counseling and the new woman, I think back to my own therapy when I was a college senior. I spent many hours in personal debate and dilemma about whether I wanted to be a career woman or a housewife. The whole conflict seemed to give me little choice when the therapist said, "Well, I wouldn't want to come home tired after a day's work and have my wife complain about her hard day at the office."†

These words illustrate the difficulty faced even now by many women who seek counseling help. Too many counselors continue to define women by their biological function and by their relationships to men, and to label them "unfeminine" when they assert themselves. It is painful for me to realize that until just a few years ago, I did the very same thing myself in my own counseling!

In 1970 a group of forty-six male and thirty-three female clinicians (psychiatrists, psychologists, and social workers) participated in an attitudinal study.‡ They were asked to complete a 122-item questionnaire which listed behaviors or traits on a bipolar basis: very subjective—very objective, very dependent—very independent, etc. The task was to indicate for each such trait whether it described a healthy male, or a

17

healthy female, or a healthy adult without regard to sex. The results were striking. Male and female clinicians alike equated healthy adult with healthy male! Healthy adult and healthy male were both seen as objective, independent, intelligent, assertive, capable. A healthy female by contrast, was seen as subjective, dependent, submissive, excitable in crisis, emotional, passive. The opinions these modern psychotherapists hold about women are remarkably like those of Freud! In the eyes of these counselors, a woman cannot be both a healthy female and a healthy adult. If she chooses to be a healthy adult, she must be "like a man." What is good for persons is not good for females.

In her classic study, *Women and Madness*, Phyllis Chesler points out that women "go crazy" more easily and oftener than men do.* Her book cites overwhelming statistics describing the greater number of women in mental hospitals and in private therapy. Probably most ministers would corroborate the statistics which indicate that more women than men ask for help. Chesler also points out that psychotherapy and marriage exercise a similar function for a woman—as vehicles for personal salvation through a benevolent male authority:

> Both psychotherapy and middle-class marriage isolate women from each other; both emphasize individual rather than collective solutions to women's unhappiness; both are based on a woman's helplessness and dependence on a stronger male authority figure. . . . Both psychotherapy and marriage enable women to express and defuse their anger by experiencing it as emotional illness, by translating it into hysterical symptoms: frigidity, chronic depression, phobias. . . . Each woman, as patient, thinks these symptoms are unique and are her own fault: she is "neurotic." She wants from a psychotherapist what she wants—and often cannot get—from a husband: attention, understanding, merciful relief, a *personal solution*— in the arms of the right husband, on the couch of the right therapist.†

Thus many women who seek counseling find little help in escaping the trap between a submissive existence in which they are of secondary importance if not actively obedient to men, and a pedestal-like existence in which they are exalted as beautiful and holy.

Increasingly, women are getting into consciousness raising groups with other women and discovering that they are not "sick," that other women have the same experiences and feelings, that they don't need counseling at all but merely a sense of their own identity which will allow them to lead fuller lives. Increasingly, too, women who do decide to enter therapy look for feminist therapists, professionals who, whether female or male, focus on helping the client define herself in terms of her own needs and potential rather than in terms of the assumptions and expectations of society or of the particular therapist about her needs.

The anger and rebelliousness women are expressing is often hard for men to understand. Men who are ministers can perhaps understand it more readily than others because they themselves sometimes feel limited as persons by other people's attitudes toward them. One male minister said well what many feel:

> I feel put in a special category by the image that many people in my congregation and community try to put on me (and it's hard not to feel it even if I don't see myself in this way).
>
> I feel both put up and put down—put on a pedestal of pseudorespect and also treated as something different, special, not fully a man.
>
> I feel that some people think I need special protection and deference (clergy discounts, exemption from the draft, clergy housing allowance, exemption from income tax), and that there's something of a put-down there, a way of saying we see you as weak and needing to be protected.
>
> I feel angry that, although my training is just as long and rigorous as that of other professionals, I am paid a lower salary.

Several male pastoral counselors of my acquaintance feel that they are viewed as lower on the totem pole than other mental health professionals with equal qualifications. Such awareness may make it easier for men counselors to understand how women feel.

Most counselors in the past have been guilty of helping *men* to stay in their boxes as well. While we have taught women to be helpless, we have taught men that to be a man means not needing help. The counselor's attitudes about being a man are as crucial to growth-producing counseling as are attitudes about being a woman.

Counseling for Wholeness

For both women and men in counseling, the question really is: "How do I become a whole person?" And that inevitably leads to another question, "What *is* a whole person?" Some psychologists are using the word *androgyny* derived from the Greek words *andros* ("male") and *gyne* ("female"), to describe the kind of wholeness that frees people to discover their full personhood.

Sandra Bem, a psychologist, has developed a scale for determining how "androgynous" an individual is.* She defines androgynous persons as those able to be either instrumental *or* expressive, assertive *or* yielding, independent *or* playful—in other words to behave appropriately as the situation requires. She found that such persons had higher overall intelligence, higher spatial ability, and greater creativity than strongly "masculine" or strongly "feminine" persons, all of whom "displayed behavioral deficits of one sort or another." The strongly "feminine" females had the greatest difficulty of all in her tests. Bem has shown that high "femininity" in females "has consistently correlated with high anxiety, low self-esteem and low social acceptance."† She also demonstrated that high "masculinity" in males is limiting though not nearly as crippling as high "femininity" in women.

These findings suggest that we live fuller lives as individuals and get along with each other better as we become more androgynous, that is, more nearly whole persons. What this means for the minister as counselor, is the importance both of striving for inner wholeness for oneself and of looking at one's counselees and parishioners as whole persons, individuals who are free to grow into whatever their own potential dictates rather than according to some arbitrary cultural or religious standards of "femininity" and "masculinity."

The issue, of course, is choice. Good counseling includes the kind of consciousness raising that helps people become aware of the options available to them. Do I choose a career in the home or out of it, or some combination of both, on the basis of my own needs and interests or because of the dictates of society? Do I choose making money and getting ahead because I want to or because of society's expectations? What other possibilities are there for me? The issue is not *what* we choose, but *that* we choose.

These concerns raise another question which is posed by the fact that most ministers who counsel with women are men. Can a male minister counsel in a liberating fashion with the women members of his congregation, who invariably make up the bulk of his counseling load? Even if he is aware of the issues, and is seriously searching for personal liberation from his own male box, can he hear the cry much less stimulate the efforts of a woman to be free?

Probably the gender of the therapist is not the crucial issue in good counseling. Many women counselors, having "made it" in a male-dominated system, have been so co-opted by the system that they see their role as that of helping their clients adjust to the respective "femininity" and "masculinity" demands of society. Certainly a woman cannot hear the cry of another woman if her own consciousness is not raised. Ideally a woman counselor with a raised consciousness, one who is struggling with her own journey toward liberation, would be a better counselor for women than a man would be and vice versa. But a liberated male counselor is better than an unliberated female counselor (for women and for men).

Some people believe that a counselor can "suspend" her or his own frame of reference while working with another person whose frame of reference is different. Thus if I am married I can help an unmarried person or if I am black I can help a white person and vice versa; age and sex too need not be barriers. I believe that this is indeed true, but only if the counselor actually sees the other person as fully human and not in some way a lesser or "not OK" person because of the difference. A heterosexual person cannot help a homosexual person to develop her or his full personhood, whatever that may mean, if the heterosexual equates homosexuality with sickness or immorality. There is no way that such a counselor could suspend that frame of reference. The same would be true where the issue is sexism: a female counselor—or a male counselor—who feels that women and men "should" learn to fit the stereotypes cannot be helpful to anybody.

A counselor can be liberating, either for women or for men, only if his or her attitude towards femaleness and maleness, toward "femininity" and "masculinity," is subjected to continuing self-examination. A person who does any kind of counseling with preconceived notions of what is best for the client, or of what the person "ought" to be and do, is not a good counselor no matter what the focus of the problem. Of course that means continually examining one's own feelings and behavior in relation to one's own "feminine" and "masculine" side: How do I relate to persons of the other sex? How is my own marriage (if I have one) affected when I truly accept the equality of the sexes? Under what circumstances do I regard my needs, especially my professional needs, as having first priority? To what extent do I feel "OK" or "not OK" about behaving in "feminine" ways (if I'm a man) or in "masculine" ways (if I'm a woman)?

The Androgynous Counselor

What, then, are the characteristics of a good counselor, an "androgynous" or liberated counselor? (By liberated, of course, I mean *relatively* liberated, one who is incessantly struggling to become liberated; no one is *completely* liberated.) Such a counselor may not be easy to find. Several characteristics of the liberated counselor can be listed. Such a counselor:

1. Values being female equally with being male. A woman counselee cannot learn to value herself from a counselor who devalues women.

2. Believes in complete equality between women and men at all levels and in all areas of public and private life, on the job, and at home.

3. Is aware of the fact that deeply imbedded cultural stereotypes are likely to have their influence on him or her at an unconscious level, even though intellectually he or she rejects such stereotypes.

4. Is nondefensive, unpretentious, and nonjudgmental.

5. Holds the basic philosophy that it is his or her job to help the client find out who she or he is and wants to be. This may mean raising the issue of other choices and options for persons who are not raising that issue for themselves.

6. Is constantly aware of his or her limitations in working with a person of the other sex.

7. Is in the process of becoming (and encouraging counselee and client to become) a more fully androgynous person.

Central to almost every religious tradition is the belief that the first humans were androgynes, beings possessed of such strength and power that the gods found it necessary to split them in half in order to preserve their own divine supremacy.* The androgynous counselor has a crucial role to play in helping us "get it all together" again as individuals and as a society. Before considering how that can happen, it is important to look at the problems and pain that the "splitting" has caused for women and men individually and in their relationships with each other.

3. Pain and Gain for Women and Men

> As men and women have been defined over against one
> another, conditioned to separateness, they have had their full
> humanity truncated, they have had their potentiality for
> genuine human communication and mutuality gravely in-
> jured.*   —Violette Lindbeck

A Rising Discontent

Across the top of the title page of a section called "Today's
Women" in a Southern California newspaper† there appeared
the pictures of nine brides (no grooms; the newspaper refuses
to print pictures of grooms). Each bride is labeled with her
husband's name—Mrs. John Jones, Mrs. Robert James, Mrs.
Peter Smith. Below the nine brides' pictures are nine articles
describing the beautiful weddings; several of them refer to the
bride as "the former Miss . . ." At the bottom of the page,
underneath the bride pictures and stories, there appears another article headlined, "Runaway Wives: Their Number is
Increasing." In this story the director of a large missing persons agency notes the statistics on runaway spouses:

> In the early 1960s . . . the number of husbands who ran
> away compared with the number of wives was about 300
> to one. By the late 1960s, the ratio had decreased to about
> 100 to one. In 1972 it was two to one. But in 1973 it was
> about even.‡

The two stories appearing on the same page made for a striking
and suggestive contrast—the beautiful brides and the runaway
wives.

There are many reasons for the discontent illustrated by
these runaway wives, among them being the rising tide of ex-

pectations and aspirations. People, especially women, are becoming aware of new options. The director of the missing persons agency mentioned above described the typical run-away wife:

> She's thirty-four-and-one-half years, married at nineteen, first child within one year of marriage, second child a year and a half later. She's intelligent, caring, anxious to elevate herself above the stereotyped roles of cook, laundress, waitress, housemaid, chauffeur.*

There was apparently a time when women in general were content with the housewife role. Some still are. But more and more women are choosing to marry late, or not at all, or to have children but not to marry, or not to have children at all. As women begin to define themselves as persons first and foremost, rather than as wives and mothers, men are also forced into new definitions of themselves. People who come to counselors these days are often struggling with these new definitions, and with the changes in lifestyles and relationships which they presage. New ways of becoming "whole" mean new kinds of problems. Ministers and pastoral counselors need to understand the old limitations and become open to the many options for being human, options to which the church in the past has been generally closed.

The Burden of Traditional Role Expectations

Two friends of mine who were expecting a baby were talking recently about their aspirations for the child soon to be born. The prospective father told of his excitement at the thought of having a son who might become a "starting forward." The other day a note came announcing the birth: of course the baby turned out to be a girl. The mother, who had been as enthusiastic as the father about having a starting forward in the family, wrote the note: "Bob is disappointed that he didn't get his starting forward but he is thrilled with our little cheerleader." The role boxes and expectations are ready and waiting even before birth!

Little boys learn early that to "be a man" means "Don't cry," "Don't fail," "Be a success," "Earn as much money as you can." Little girls learn to be sweet, pretty, and not too smart, and never to beat a boy at anything. Limit youself to cheering him along from the sidelines. In our culture we teach boys from the outset to develop an independent sense of self, and that is good. We teach girls to develop a capacity for intimate relationships, and that is also good. What we do not do, most of the time, is to teach boys and girls to become both independent *and* interdependent, that is, to find strength both in themselves *and* in their relationships.

Adolescent girls are even now expected to curb further any signs of independence or assertiveness, to let boys take the initiative in activities and in dating, and to think of marriage and children as their most important goal. Increasingly young women are choosing education and career, but frequently only as something to do in case they don't get married. Boys are expected to choose a job or career and decide how they will earn money for the rest of their lives. They are expected to be the aggressor when it comes to relationships with girls. Girls thus learn to get what they want by subterfuge and manipulation. At this age, as at earlier ones, we do not encourage boys and girls to look at a variety of options with respect to both relationships and occupations. We hurry both sexes into marriage, parenting, and breadwinning.

It is still true that most men and women marry and become parents. Instead of expanding the personal horizons of both partners, marriage too often means limiting them. Women find themselves isolated and lonely, burdened with house and children. Men often find themselves trapped in jobs they don't enjoy, caught up in the achievement rat race, and burdened with the perpetual responsibility of supporting the family. Children get too much mother, not enough father. Husbands and wives grow distant; no wonder one or the other runs away. We emphasize too heavily the joys of motherhood without noting its frustrations. We do the opposite for men; we focus more on the burdens than on the satisfactions of fatherhood.

Women who decide to pursue a job or career outside the home, whether by choice or by necessity, (more than one-

third of the U.S. work force is composed of women) often feel
guilty about neglecting their children; they also resent being
overloaded with two jobs, one at home and one away. Some
women who actually choose to be a homemaker now feel a
new inner conflict; they think they hear the collective voice of
the women's movement saying that the role of housewife and
mother is "not OK." Thus women may feel a double bind—
traditional society telling them to stay home, the new consciousness telling them to get out.

Married women approaching middle age often face a new
set of problems. If they have accepted society's dictum and
defined themselves almost exclusively around their roles as
mothers and wives they may find it difficult to see what the
future holds for them when their children leave home. In
Doris Lessing's *Summer Before the Dark* Kate Brown antici-
pates the departure of her youngest child: "She felt like a
long-term prisoner who is going to have to face freedom in the
morning."*

Menopause is traumatic for many women. Besides the new
and surprising physical symptoms and changes it brings, which
vary greatly from woman to woman, women often fear also
the loss of their "sex appeal" (as defined by the cultural stereotype). A woman has to deal not only with her own feelings
about the change and the passage of time but also with the
dehumanizing attitude of society toward the menopausal
woman.†

Middle-aged men face different problems. If they have
achieved the goals they once set for themselves, or had set for
them, they may be happy in their work but feel that they have
grown apart from their wives and distant from their children.
Or they may have struggled long and hard for a goal which
continues to elude them and seems more distant than ever as
middle age approaches. Both groups of men fall into the
category of "high risk" for heart attacks.

Old age hits women and men somewhat differently. Large
numbers of women are widows, faced not only with aging but
with aging alone and in isolation. Or they may be confronted
with the demands of a retired husband who is suddenly at

home all the time with nothing to do. Although old age in our society is generally viewed negatively for both sexes, the negative image of the older woman as the "little old lady" is far more common than any comparable image for the older man, who is often regarded as "distinguished" or "wise." Older men are more in demand than older women, partly because there are fewer of them. Nonetheless, men who have made it successfully through middle age may face at retirement the "cold wind from the future"* that women faced when their children grew up and left home. Because of our society's attitude toward nonproductiveness, retirement may be a severe blow for a man. If his entire adult life has revolved around the "male machine" mystique, if he has not developed warm and close relationships and absorbing interests outside the productive world of job or career, retirement may feel to him like the end. Some men do in fact just curl up and die. In this way, aging may be easier for women, who are more apt to have learned to find satisfaction in relationships.

Single people are severely dehumanized by the cultural norm which defines people as successful only if they marry. Women feel the pressure to marry even more strongly than men; even those who have chosen singleness and feel happier than their married friends seem to be, or who have achievements to their credit equal to those of men, are generally considered to be "unfulfilled." Divorced women are often made to feel the added pressure of having "failed" at the most important job for a woman; they may have full responsibility for raising the children, and even be supporting the family, but they are still regarded as "a failure."

Although the image of the single or divorced man is a much more desirable one, men too face the problems of singleness to some extent. Divorced men often have heavy financial burdens, and sometimes are cut off from their children by circumstances and customs which favor the mother in custody proceedings.

Probably the heaviest burden for single people in a couple-oriented society is loneliness. Because we live in a culture in which things are supposed to come out even, the single person in a group of married people is uncomfortable and so are the couples who often feel they must find a "partner" for the single one. Churches are probably as guilty as any institution of slighting the single person both in attitudes and in activities.

New Options

One of the spin-offs of the rising consciousness of women— and therefore of men—is that it is not only OK to be single but it can be a highly desirable and fulfilling lifestyle for many people. Marriage isn't the only place to get one's relationship needs met. Both the married and the single state have their advantages; again, the crucial issue is choice and the fullest opportunity for every individual to be and to become fully human.

The rising divorce rate suggests the need for a kind of counseling that can help a couple to separate creatively. Of course that means encouraging them to look at the factors which got them into the marriage and those which are forcing them out. It means helping them to deal with anger and hostility so that the children do not become pawns, to work out the legal problems amicably, and to do their grief work thoroughly. But the main focus of divorce counseling is to encourage both women and men to see themselves as whole people still, with the potential of a satisfying life ahead whether they marry again or not.

Although it often follows, divorce counseling is *not* the same as marriage counseling. Divorce counseling is based on the assumption that it may be better for some couples to separate, rather than on the traditional attitude of the church that a marriage must be saved if possible and that divorce is always a tragedy. A divorce may be the most humanizing option if a particular couple got married for all the wrong reasons in the first place or if one or both persons would be better off single. Divorce counseling is a kind of counseling and consciousness raising that affirms singleness as an option for human wholeness.

There are a number of issues connected directly or indirectly with sexuality around which both women and men are struggling today. Women are learning from new research and are discovering for themselves that they can accept and enjoy their long repressed sexuality. For many women that means dealing with guilt, because they have been brought up to believe that "nice girls don't" take the initiative, or even enjoy sex. Often it also means frustration. Long repressed sexuality is sometimes hard to call forth. Becoming "orgasmic," to say nothing of "multiply orgasmic" is not easy when one has been taught to accept, even to cultivate, "frigidity." For men, "the new woman" may at first appear sexually threatening when it develops that she sometimes likes to take the initiative and can actually have more orgasms than he can. Ultimately, however, as members of both sexes escape the sexual double standards, learn about their bodies and what they like, and come to enjoy being both receptive and aggressive, tender as well as tendered to, sex becomes more humanizing for both.

As lifestyles broaden, more and more people are enjoying sex outside of marriage. Premarital sex has its values if it keeps people from getting married who otherwise would get married only for the sake of having sex. Also, as more and more people decide not to marry, sex for single people is an increasingly practiced, and accepted, phenomenon. As a society we have no right to deny the joys of sex to people who do not marry, or who marry late by choice or by necessity, or who have lost a mate by death or divorce.

Another increasingly viable lifestyle for many people as we broaden our perspective on what it means to be human, is that of homosexuality. A young woman said to me recently that she stays away from her church and her minister because she knows her lifestyle would be unacceptable—she would be told she was a sinner. Ministers and counselors could be influential in changing attitudes which make a person feel less than human simply because she or he behaves differently from the majority.*

Humanizing or "liberating" sex is that which affirms the full personhood of both participants. Whether in marriage or out of it, whether between the sexes or within the sexes, it says that sex is good, and that our bodies are good, provided that neither participant treats the other as an object meant chiefly for gratification.

Dehumanizing aspects of sex can be found within marriage as well as out of it. The crucial attitude for the minister is a nonjudgmental one which helps people look at the sexual aspects of their relationships in the same way they look at other aspects, that is, with a view to what is most humanizing for both parties. An awareness and appreciation of new attitudes toward sexual satisfaction, attitudes which are humanizing to both women and men, is important for ministers and counselors who want to work with people in this area, and who want to change the all-too-common attitude that the church is "against" sex. At the same time ministers and the church can have a profound influence on the development in individuals and in society of attitudes toward sex which are in fact humanizing and not exploitative.

There are three other related situations in which women are often asking for help these days—pregnancy outside of marriage, abortion, and rape. Ministers and counselors can be helpful at such times only if they are truly open to the options women face in those circumstances, and truly willing to help counselees deal with their feelings and decide for *themselves* what is best for them. Women in any of those circumstances need to be encouraged to talk to other women who have had like experiences and/or are trained to help. Women's health centers and rape crisis centers are excellent agencies for referrals. Of course people are not likely to discuss their concerns in the area of sexuality with any minister or counselor whom they perceive to be judgmental about their thoughts and behavior.*

Pains and Gains

Many of us women, when we first begin to recognize the restrictions which define us in terms of physical attractiveness and our relationships to men, respond with intense anger; this initial response is frequently followed by serious steps to find new directions. Others of us react first of all with fear— which may account for the remarkable phenomenon of "pussy cat" and "fascinating woman" programs that encourage women to be "feminine" with a vengeance, to subordinate themselves entirely to men, and get what they want through dishonest manipulation. Such an approach generally appeals to people who are more comfortable with authoritarian guide- lines. On the whole, however, women are pushing for equal- ity, for recognition, for a share in the power, for men to take more responsibility in matters of family life, child raising, and home maintenance. The pain women feel revolves around anger at their long and usually unconscious imprisonment *and* around the fear that they might now have to get out of the accustomed boxes.

As men get past their angry resistance to the demands of women, and as they become aware of the pain caused by the traditional definition of "masculinity," they too begin to raise questions. The strong, superior and aggressive male image is a safe, rewarding, and powerful one. Many men find it diffi- cult and threatening even to think of sharing the power which has so long been theirs in personal, social, economic, and po- litical life. It is hard to believe that there may be gains to be had from such a change. Even when a man discovers that he likes the new and more vulnerable side of himself, he may find that others reject him.

Nevertheless, many men are now discovering the gains which can result from the current changes in female-male identities. They are even articulating them in men's con- sciousness raising groups:

> I wanted to explore my feelings and compare my changing thinking about masculinity with what other men my age were thinking.

> Belonging to this group has been a most rewarding experience. I have found men to whom I can relate feelings that I have never revealed to anyone else. At times I have become angry, but I have talked my anger out. Because of the group, I have had discussions with my wife instead of quarrels.

> This was my first experience of "rapping" with other men about intimate problems. . . . Learning that other men feel the same as I do helps me to clarify my own problems.
>
> I learned that I can be honest about my feelings. If I'm hurt, it's OK to cry.
>
> I now realize that I can react according to my feelings—I don't have to be the logical man all the time.
>
> In five years I'd like to be living on the land, working part-time and able to take the time to reflect and to map my inner space.
>
> In five years I'd like to be leading a lifestyle similar to my present one, but I'd like to work less, vacation more, love and be loved.*

The last two comments reflect a growing awareness among men that they want something more than simply financial or job success. That is surely a gain which can lead to a decrease in the heart attack rate now so high among middle-aged men, as well as to more humanizing relationships.

As women and men get out of their boxes and begin to discover their full selves, as individuals with potential far beyond the traditional "feminine" and "masculine" stereotypes, the possibilities for personal growth will be far more varied and exciting. The potential for enriched human relationships between women and men will likewise increase. Counselors can do more than observe these changes in role stereotypes; they can encourage them and help people build on them.

4. Counseling Amid Changing Relationships

There is a tendency to overlook interdependency as a part of healthy human relations, both those of husband and wife and also those of people in general.*   —Mabel Blake Cohen

All the studies of middle-class marriages show that companionship, the hallmark of the egalitarian marriage, is one of the most important ingredients for a successful marriage, especially for the wife, no matter what criterion or index is used to measure success.†   —Jessie Bernard

Marriage in Transition

It is likely that we have thus far seen only the tip of the iceberg in the upheaval in relationships between women and men. Marriage relationships are especially vulnerable and responsive to changing roles and identities. More and more marriages will feel the pain and the excitement of change. It may be that the divorce rate will rise even higher as couples struggle unsuccessfully to develop more satisfying marriage styles. At the same time many couples will succeed in discovering the gains in more egalitarian and companionable marriages. Counselors of all disciplines can have a positive role in helping to redefine the institution of marriage and in helping couples to develop creative and growth-producing relationships.

The Dominance/Submission Pattern in Marriage

Connie and Steve had come for their first visit to a marriage counselor. Steve has described their problem in a nutshell: after five years of marriage Connie just "dropped the bomb" —she suddenly decided she wanted to do her own thing. Although he found it difficult, he has adjusted to her returning

34

to school and to a job, and to his having to share the house-work and child care.

STEVE: But it still isn't enough. She's still not satisfied. I don't know what she wants. I'm doing everything she's asked. She can't even tell me what she wants. She keeps saying she wants me to talk to her. I talk to her all the time! I don't know what she means, and she can't seem to tell me.

CONNIE: I don't *know* what I want, exactly. It's more than just talking to me, just letting me do whatever I want, just having things run smoothly without any conflict. There must be more to marriage than the day in, day out routine, even when it's shared. I guess I want Steve to tell me what his real feelings are, what he wants out of life. I don't know—it's hard to put into words. I don't even know if I love him anymore!

COUNSELOR: (to Steve) That must be pretty hard to take.

STEVE: Damn right it is! Of course she loves me. She's just got this crazy idea in her head that she wants to live her own life, and that doesn't include me—in spite of the fact that I've made every possible concession to her.

COUNSELOR: (to Connie) Steve is pretty angry with you.

CONNIE: Yes, and I don't blame him. I *have* upset everything and he *has* given in to what I wanted, even when he didn't like doing it. I *appreciate* that. I don't know how to say what it is that's missing. Maybe it's just that I married him for the wrong reasons—security and all that—and we aren't really compatible. We don't seem to want to talk about the same things or do the same things together anymore.

When some of the anger and frustration had been dealt with, not only verbally but also physically using foam rubber bats,* and Connie and Steve were feeling a little more friendly toward each other, the counselor asked them to try telling each other what they still liked about their marriage and about each other. She asked them each to complete the sentence, "I appreciate in you . . ." as many times as they could. They found that, in spite of the anger and distance between them, there were still some things they liked about each other.

Then the counselor asked them, in turn, to complete the sentence, "I need from you . . ." as many times as they could.

CONNIE: I need from you more understanding and tolerance of my need to be independent. I need from you more flexibility in letting the children just be themselves without always telling them what boys should do and what girls should do. I need you to tell me what worries you and what you're afraid of. I need you to tell me when things don't go well on your job. I need you to be willing to talk about painful things sometimes and not pretend to yourself that everything's OK when it isn't. I need you to share with me what you really care about—or maybe to find out what it is you care about.

Connie was fighting back tears by this time and saying that she found it very hard to put into words what her needs were. Steve's needs were for more and better sex, for her to stop avoiding him, for her to be more affectionate, for her to show that she loved him.

Connie and Steve illustrate one kind of struggle that many marriages are facing these days. The "unconscious contract" under which they married called for dominance on the part of Steve and submission from Connie. She didn't even know how to drive a car when she got married. She was dependent on Steve for transportation, earning money, and even bailing her out at home when the demands became too great. Steve was competent and successful at everything he did and enjoyed "taking care of" Connie. When she began to change, first by learning to drive, then by making new friends; developing interests of her own, and going back to school and to work, Steve was angry. He resisted each new development. But he was also a little bit proud; probably that little bit of pride—and the fact that they basically liked each other—is what has held them together. But now their needs seem no longer to overlap. The task for Connie and Steve is to sort out whether they simply do not have enough in common anymore to make possible a mutually satisfying marriage, or whether it is simply that her rebelliousness toward the old ways and his resistance to the new ones are still getting in the way. The counselor's job is to help them discover whether Connie's needs for a deeper kind of communication can also become Steve's needs and whether they have enough in common to build a relationship with a different, more conscious and articulated "contract."

Connie and Steve's relationship is an extreme (though not uncommon) example of the dominance-submission pattern in marriage. Nevertheless, their relationship had more strengths than many. Connie discovered her inner strength as she became more aware of her limited life, and Steve discovered his as she began to challenge their lifestyle. Not all marriages get that far. Some women become increasingly depressed and end up hospitalized or at least on the psychiatrist's couch; some women simply get angry and leave before they have a chance to discover whether change can occur in the marriage. Men too sometimes get angry and seek divorce before taking time to discover whether there could be some gains for them in a new style of relating.

Variations on the Pattern

There are variations on the dominance-submission pattern. Sometimes it is the man who is "weak" and the woman who takes the active leadership role, either subtly or overtly. Some couples are quite happy with this arrangement. It fits their own needs and personalities, and they have the strength to live that way even though society may say it's "unnatural." Often, though, because of their inner conflicts or because of the dictates of society, couples find themselves in conflict, not only with each other but also with their expectations of themselves.

June and Mark came to the counselor when they were considering divorce because of Mark's sexual impotence and his

inability to hold a job. Conflict had reached the point at
which hostility was never absent; they could see little or nothing good about their relationship.

JUNE: He's such a dud. He can't even keep a job. It's not
because he isn't *smart*—he just won't apply himself. He
just doesn't care about me and the children. I want to get
my old job back—I made good money before we were
married—but Mark won't hear of it.

MARK: If she'd just leave me alone, I'd be all right. It's her
constant nagging and pushing that I don't like. I'm just
never going to be a company president. I don't want to be.
And when I begin to get settled and happy in a job she keeps
asking why I'm satisfied where I am. Why can't *she* be
satisfied if *I* am? And she wants sex all the time too. No
wonder I'm impotent when she's so pushy.

The temptation here is to get involved in a Freudian analysis of why Mark and June were led into such an "unnatural"
reversal of roles. What is important from the standpoint of
consciousness raising and counseling is to widen one's perspective as a counselor on what is in fact "masculine," and
what "feminine." June and Mark may discover for themselves that their personalities are *right for them*, even though
they are at variance with the stereotypes sanctioned by society.
   In the course of the counseling, as they began to explore
their relationship, June found that much of her pushiness and
hostility was an attempt to get Mark to "make a woman of
me"; she recognized her feelings of inadequacy as a woman
who was strong and assertive when she "should" be soft and
"feminine." Mark came to realize that he resisted June's
pushiness not only because it didn't fit his idea of what a
woman "ought" to be, but also because it reinforced his feeling of not being a "real man."
   Counseling helped June and Mark to sort out which was
their "pathology"—the extent to which Mark was out of touch
with his assertive and aggressive side and June out of touch

with her soft and gentle side, and the extent to which their feelings and conflicts were simply their reaction to a society which does not affirm a "passive" male and an "aggressive" female. When each began to assess the sort of persons they really were and wanted to be, they decided that June was more ambitious and Mark more content to take life as it comes. June went back to her job where instead of pushing Mark she could push herself to get ahead. Mark found himself content in a nondemanding job where he didn't need to get ahead and could have more time for his children and for just "puttering around." At last report, they both were happy with the new relationship, including its sexual side—Mark was no longer impotent.

The "Sibling" Marriage Pattern

An increasingly common problem in counseling is that of the young couple married five to ten years who are fairly comfortable with each other but realize that the "spark" has gone out of their relationship.

Art and Linda had been married ten years and had a five-year-old child. They came for help because of Linda's increasing dissatisfaction with life. Art had his own business, which was growing. Linda was a secretary with an excellent job. Money was not a problem.

LINDA: I don't understand what I'm unhappy about. I can't really complain about Art. He's a good husband and father. He does his share of the housework and parenting. He doesn't limit me in any way, except maybe he doesn't enjoy having fun as much as I do. He has a good job and makes good money. Other women think I'm crazy, that I don't really appreciate what I've got. And they're right.

ART: Damn right they are!

LINDA: But sometimes it seems as though there must be more to life than this. Here I am at twenty-eight an old married woman. We got married right out of high school, you know. and we'd been going together two years then. We

just sort of drifted into marriage and having a child—and
now it's more like we're brother and sister. I like Art and
I don't want to hurt him. But somehow everything is just
the same old daily routine. It's dull . . .

ART: The only thing I can see wrong with our marriage is that
our sex life isn't as good as it used to be. Linda doesn't get
turned on very often anymore. She wants more romance
and excitement. But, hell, I'm the same person I always
was. And I love her. We don't fight—I can't see that
there are even any issues between us except that she feels
like my sister. Sheesh! No wonder she doesn't like sex.

Linda subsequently found, as her consciousness about herself rose, that she had never explored the options open to her
as a person before she married—a variety of relationships,
education, maybe even travel. Now the relationship with Art
seemed stifling. The situation of Linda and Art is an increasingly common one, and a difficult and painful result of the
rising consciousness of women. It will be a difficult struggle
to find out whether Linda can get her needs for broader horizons met and still stay with Art. Marriage for Linda was
originally a mere extension of the security of her childhood
home. She is a good example of the risk involved when a
young girl is taught to define herself in terms of the man she
will marry. Art illustrates the limitations of the kind of young
male identity formation which allows a man to be content with
a good job, a good home, a good wife, and good children,
without ever considering the possibility of a deeper relationship with a woman as a person. A generation ago, even now
in many cases, a marriage like Linda's and Art's would rarely
come into question. But rising expectations, especially those
of women, are now turning apparently stable and unconflicted
marriages into battlegrounds. Linda could easily become a
"runaway wife."

The Child-Child Marriage Pattern

Another version of the "sibling" marriage is the one in
which two demanding "children" are struggling to get their

needs met. Each is so deprived that neither can meet the needs of the other. Such relationships are usually characterized by bickering, distancing, and hurting behavior on the part of both. Depending on how severe the pathology, a consciousness raising experience for the woman sometimes presages improvement in the marriage.

Bob and Phyllis were on the verge of divorce when they came for counseling. Neither had anything good to say about the other. Besides ongoing marriage counseling directed toward draining off the anger and discovering whether there was anything salvageable in the marriage, the counselor—in this instance a man—recommended a consciousness raising group for Phyllis. She attended faithfully and began to discover her identity as a person and a woman instead of a helpless child. As she brought back to the marriage and to the counseling sessions her growing self-awareness, she began both to confront Bob with his male chauvinism and at the same time to let him know she was aware that he was as trapped as she was.

At this point the counselor asked them to join a couples therapy group where they both received affirmation of their strengths and confrontation about their childish behavior. It would have been even better if Bob could have found a men's consciousness raising group too. Unfortunately none was available. Nonetheless, the combination of consciousness raising for Phyllis, and conjoint counseling followed by a growth-therapy group for couples helped Bob and Phyllis learn to value each other and themselves as adults, and to find new and more constructive ways of dealing with their conflicts.

The Mid-Years Marriage

Another kind of relationship which often is struggling to survive or to come alive is the marriage of fifteen to twenty-five years duration. Here the conflict is often triggered by the children leaving home and the wife finding that she needs to make a new life for herself. Sometimes she finds it with a vengeance (I speak from my own experience)* and the changes she demands after twenty years of a "satellite marriage" are deeply threatening to the marriage. Although the

middle-years couple has been married longer than those described earlier, and therefore are more "set in their ways," the
issues aroused and the approaches called for are much the
same.

Minority Culture Marriages

There is perhaps another sort of relationship which is beginning to suffer (or to grow) under the influence of the changing consciousness of women, and that is the marriage best
described as the machismo male and the submissive female
couple. Such marriages are found in all segments of our society but may be more common among minority cultures where
men are almost as dehumanized by the white male dominant
culture as are women. In these instances the man is usually
free to do as he pleases and expects the woman to do as *he*
pleases too. Women in such marriages are often there because
they were not aware of other choices.

A young Chicano of my acquaintance remarked one day
when we were talking about the options for young girls in her
culture:

> The female role of getting married right out of high school—
> a lot of my cousins, a lot of people I know, have done this—
> it's not something that's explicitly said to the female. *It's
> kind of in the air.*

This young woman was a college student, clearly challenging
the mores of her culture and feeling resistance from her family
and friends. She hoped for marriage eventually, but of a
different kind than that sanctioned by her subculture.

Some men in minority cultures are finding, as they move
into the middle-class world through job or profession, that
friendship between women and men is possible and that a
companionship marriage can be more satisfying than the one
they have grown up with and married into. Often in such
instances it is difficult for the woman who is content with the
old way to "keep up" with a husband who begins asking her to
go places with him, to read books and discuss ideas, and to

make new kinds of friends, when her satisfaction and security are chiefly in home and family.

Contemporary Marriage Counseling

A full-blown discussion of marriage counseling is beyond the scope of the present book. However, some mention of those aspects of marriage counseling which are particularly related to current changes in roles and identities is important.

The Marriage Contract in Counseling

One excellent form of consciousness raising for both pre-wedding and post-wedding couples of all ages is to encourage them to write a marriage contract or covenant. A marriage contract is a good device for helping a couple to enrich a marriage that is reasonably stable and satisfying, or to reassess a marriage that is in trouble. The purpose of such an exercise, written or verbal, is to bring the unconscious contract under which most couples marry to a conscious level where they have some choice about it.

Over the centuries, couples entering into marriage have committed themselves in one way or another to the partner whom they have agreed to marry. Such contracts have ranged all the way from onesided commitments involving a dowry and bride price to the more spiritual commitment to "love, honor, and cherish" or "love, honor, and obey." Consciously "spelled-out-on-paper" contracts about who will earn the money, raise the children, and do the housework are becoming more common. Education for marriage and pre-marriage counseling provides an opportunity for young people not yet ready for commitment—as well as for those thinking about or planning marriage—to study possible options and to identify and articulate their own hopes and expectations for marriage as well as what they expect and want from the person they marry.

Some contracts are elaborate. They may even be legally drawn. They often include provisions about religious practices for the couple and for any children who may arrive; whether or not they plan to have children; what they will do in the case of a pregnancy not wanted by one or the other; what will happen if the couple decides to separate; what the financial arrangements will be in such a case; what provision will be made for the children; how in-laws, relatives, and friends will be included in the relationship; what sexual practices will be followed; under what circumstances the couple will move from one home to another; whose job will take precedence; and what kinds of freedom each partner is to have.

Some such conscious agreement, whether written or verbal, is essential in a time of changing expectations. It can no longer be assumed that each partner will fall into a prescribed role in marriage. Too many couples discover *after* the fact that he expected her to give up her job while she expected to keep it, or vice versa; that she planned for her mother to live with them, while he didn't; that he wanted several children, while she didn't want any; that she expected him to take out the garbage, while he thought that was a woman's job. Any form of premarriage or marriage counseling or enrichment these days should encourage a couple to look at their expectations both about the routine details of everyday living (like the garbage) and their expectations about the long-range issues involved in any relationship.

Such discussion and contracting, both written and spoken, would also need to include provisions for reevaluating and recontracting at various points in the relationship and to plan for how and when to do it. The couple might want to join a growth group, create an ongoing support group with other couples, get the professional help of a third party at particular points, or simply plan to review their contract at each anniversary and get help if they seem to need it. Expectations, needs and interests change with the passage of time. It is crucial to help a couple both before marriage and after it to be flexible in their contracting, to revise the contract regularly, and to feel committed to keeping the contract.

Dealing with Sexuality in Counseling

Among the many problems that couples and individuals of both sexes present to counselors in these days of greater openness are those of sexual dysfunction. *Dysfunction* is a sort of scary word covering everything from impotence and premature ejaculation on the part of the man and frigidity on the part of the woman to differing needs in the area of sex. Some couples don't get along in that area because one wants more sex and the other less, or they have different views about who should take the initiative, or they are just too mad at each other to enjoy sex, or one is interested in swinging and the other is not. All these and a variety of other problems are coming to be included under the umbrella term "sexual dysfunction."

Along with the rise in the incidence of such problems (or perhaps it is simply the rising expectation that sex "should" be enjoyable), the development of sex therapy methods and the generally greater freedom to talk about the subject openly, there has also been an increase in the number of sex therapy clinics and counselors. Some of these are simply irresponsible operations taking advantage of a fad. Others are reputable clinics involving individuals who have had both specific training in the new therapies and sound experience in dealing both with sexual dysfunction and with all other inseparably related aspects of the female-male relationships. Before referring couples for sex therapy, or before focusing on sex specifically as "the problem," a counselor needs to explore with the couple their total relationship. Very often, sexual dysfunction clears up as other problems in the relationship are resolved—and vice versa, of course.

Ministers and counselors can help couples having sexual difficulties.* Counselees who are changing their style of relationship to a more egalitarian one can be helped to realize that, if they are having new sexual problems, this is not unusual and is even to be expected. When a relationship changes in one area, it changes in other areas too. If a couple is working out a new way to get the housework done on a more shared basis, they may have to work out new ways to enjoy sex as well.

When relationships between women and men are changing, anger between the sexes is inevitable. A minister or counselor can help couples to deal constructively with anger that is also getting in the way of good sex. Couples can be helped to learn to talk to each other about sex, to show each other what they like, to take time together to enjoy each other physically, to try different settings and different techniques, but mainly to see sex as a part of a total relationship which cannot be good if other areas are not also good.

Jessie Bernard asks whether equality and good sex go together.* She concludes that although good sex may be more difficult during the period of transition to equality there is no inherent reason why sex has to be a dominance-submission game; it can eventually be much more satisfying in a relationship of equality. Counselors can encourage couples to stick it out in that area instead of giving up before they discover what the possibilities are.

Changing Expectations

Recently there were reported in a Southern California newspaper the results of a national opinion survey.† Of the 3000 women polled, 96 percent still viewed marriage as their first choice for the most satisfying and interesting way of life. What is changing is the *kind* of marriage these women look forward to. Sixty-one percent of women under thirty favor a marriage of equal partnership, where husband and wife both work outside the home and share homemaking and child care responsibilities. Half of all college women of any age favor such a marriage. An increasing percentage of women view the single life as a satisfying one if such a marriage is not possible. And 61 percent of all women polled found divorce acceptable if the marriage is bad. Only 40 percent see having children as an important reason for getting married. Even more recent statistics published by the U.S. Census Bureau indicate that an increasing number of young persons are thinking twice about marriage. The number of persons between 25 and 34 years of age who had never been married had increased by 50 percent in only 5 years. In the same period the percentage of persons between 25 and 54 who had been married and were divorced and not remarried jumped from 7 to 10. Families with women as the only adult jumped from 1.6 million to 7.2 million in the same 5 years.*

Clearly the "traditional" marriage in which it is automatically assumed that the man will earn the money and be more or less dominant and the woman will raise the children and be more or less submissive—which has been and still is the commonest pattern in Western society—is changing. It is obviously no longer enough to support and encourage the institution of marriage without raising some questions about what we mean by marriage. There is no simple answer anymore to what marriage is or ought to be.

It is important for the counselor when working with couples to keep in mind that the new ethic of equality between the sexes in marriage does not mean there is some kind of new blueprint for what a marriage ought to be like. If the broadening of options in our society continues, as it seems likely to do, then equal partnership will mean different things for different people. The "traditional" way will continue to be an option, so long as it is a conscious *choice*. However, it will likely be characterized by the added factor that the sex roles will be reversible—the man may choose to stay home and the woman to earn the money. What will *not* be an option is the unbalanced "His" and "Hers" marriage in which the woman "dwindles" into a wife and the man "enlarges" into a husband.†

The examples in this chapter have illustrated various situations in which marriages are in trouble largely because of tight role expectations or because of the changing consciousness of the woman or the man. Of course couples come for counseling and enrichment for lots of other reasons too. But it is always wise to explore the possible connections between any presenting problem and the question of changing roles. Helping women and men to get out of their boxes frees them to discover themselves as individuals in their full humanity, and then to discover what they really want and need in a relationship.

When they are consulted in time counselors can help couples explore the nature and implications of the marriage patterns, expectations, and contracts with which they have been operating. One great advantage that ministers and pastoral counselors have is the opportunity for education and consciousness raising about changing roles and identities and their effect on marriage through other facets of church life. When people are aware of a minister's open attitude in these controversial areas they are more apt to come to her or him for help before it is too late.

5. Liberating the Church

Silam . . . "the inhabitant or soul (*inua*) of the universe," is never seen; its voice alone is heard. "All we know is that it has a gentle voice like a woman, a voice 'so fine and gentle that even children cannot become afraid.' What it says is: *sila ersinarsinivdluge*, 'be not afraid of the universe.' "*
—Najagnek, an Eskimo of North Alaska

Discontent and Discovery

For most of us women and men who have grown up in a world where men are the image makers and decision makers and where even God is male, it comes as a surprise to discover that, offstage, the figure of a woman looms large. In the first volume of *The Masks of God*, Joseph Campbell remarks:

For it is one of the curiosities and difficulties of our subject that its materials come to us for the most part through the agency of the male. The masters of the rites, the sages and prophets, and lastly our contemporary scholars of the subject, have usually been men; whereas, obviously, there has always been a feminine side to the picture also. The symbols have been experienced and read from the two poles; but also shaped from the force of the two poles in their antagonistic cooperation. So that even where the woman may seem to have disappeared from the scene—as, for example, in the patriarchal Aranda and Hebrew images of the first days of creation—we must realize that she is there, even so, and watch for the ripple of her presence behind the curtain.†

Ministers need to know about many women's growing awareness of their present position in the church and of their religious and cultural heritage. The pastoral counselor in particular needs to be personally interested and professionally concerned in order to be able to minister effectively to women who are feeling alienated from the church and seeking change, as well as to women who are resistant to or feel threatened by the changes some women are seeking. Ministers and pastoral counselors also need to be able to interpret to the men of the church what it is that many women are feeling and seeking, and to interpret to the church the importance of revaluing the "feminine" in God and in theology.

Here are some words one woman wrote following a worship service:

> I sit in church today alternately smoldering with anger, fighting back tears of hurt and regret, and grasping at those elusive moments when I can truly affirm the experience of worship. Because suddenly I feel left out. "Once to Every Man and Nation," "O Brother Man," "How Shall a Rich man . . . ," "Rise Up, O Men of God," and on and on and on. Lots of male words; no female ones.
>
> Except for some women in the choir there are only men in the service—in the pulpit, at the altar, in the aisles. There are mostly women in the pews.
>
> We've turned to another hymn, "Open My Eyes." Here's where the tears want to come. At last I can really sing. In this one God is a spirit, not a man. And there are no words that call only the men and not the women. I wish people *would* open their eyes and see what I am seeing.
>
> The sermon is talking about ethical issues for mankind. "Every man ought to have an equal chance." (Women too?) Finally the preacher mentions a woman but she is "only a midwife."
>
> It is time for the last hymn, "Turn Back, O Man." Ha! There's an admonition I don't have to heed. It's not talking to me! Oddly enough as the stanzas wear on, the first significant mention of the female occurs. *Earth* and *nature* are both labeled "she." The existence of the female side of the universe is at last recognized.

This expression of one woman's feelings about the worship experience describes the feelings of a growing number of women in the church, including many who have spent a lifetime there. Many of us are learning to identify the sources of our discontent.

Beyond that, however, we are also learning to translate the

anger and hurt we first feel with that kind of awareness into a search for another side of the story. We are listening to feminist theologians who are calling for a new theology which will express and affirm the experience of women as well as of men. We are learning about the "feminine in divinity," a concept long missing from the traditional emphasis on God as Father, Lord, and King. We are discovering the days when God was a woman, and the "symphony of hymns . . . to the Great Goddess" which is sung in myth and religious tradition all around the earth.* We are discovering Bible mistranslations which changed "children" into "sons," and "people" into "men." We are learning about women in history, both individual women whose contributions have been ignored or forgotten, and the masses of women in all cultures and periods of history who have had tremendous influence on the evolution of human society, from the invention of agriculture to the "keeping of the faith."

We are becoming aware of a whole body of data accumulated within the last one hundred years which has stirred the flames of controversy in religious, anthropological, and philosophical circles—data that raises new questions about the origins of the family and of human society. We are learning about matrifocal cultures in which descent may be through the woman's family, in which the mother-child relationship is the important social unit and women have great prestige and sometimes political power. Data about such societies raise lots of fascinating questions about whether society began with patriarchy—which has long been the prevalent assumption— or whether there was once a universally benevolent and egalitarian society which revolved around the mother as the human representative of the Mother Goddess Earth, the goddess who remains with us to this day in the figure of Mother Nature. Questions about the origin of the family and of human society are not yet answered, and may never be, but they are serious questions now being dealt with enthusiastically in several disciplines.† Women who allow themselves to get in touch with the feelings that accompany such discontent in the church first get angry. But if they go on from the anger to try to discover the "other side of the story" they get excited. It is a profoundly life-affirming experience for a woman to learn that she has a historical and religious heritage heretofore largely ignored. For many of us it is as though we have discovered a whole new identity.

First we "try it on for size." How does it feel to think of God as Mother as well as or instead of Father? We try to get together with other women who are having the same feelings. Maybe we try to have the minister consider changing the church language and literature to make it more inclusive. Or we may try to get the church to include women in its life and leadership in more important ways than it has in the past. If we do not succeed, we may turn to or even organize a feminist church, where our spiritual needs can be met and we can feel ourselves an integral part of the tradition and practice. Some women struggle and even manage to survive in the traditional church on Sunday morning by changing the words in the liturgy and hymns to female words—Father to Mother, King to Queen, Him to Her—when speaking of God.* However we handle it, we are making a deep and vital change in our own sense of identity and asking the church to change as well.

Inevitable Resistance

On the other hand, many women in the church are resistant to the changing status of women. Often they are critical of women in the professional ministry, or of women challenging the traditional roles of women in the church. Sometimes they resist because they feel that the contribution they are making to church life, and have made in the past, is being belittled. Sometimes they resist because they fear, usually unconsciously, the kind of new responsibilites they may have to take up if women should come to share equally in the wider life of church and society.

An enlightened minister or pastoral counselor can help such women to become aware that whatever they have done in the past is not being criticized but affirmed, and that the changes called for don't necessarily mean that women are being asked to give up the roles they now hold. Women who are frightened or resistant can be helped to understand that the issue is simply one of choice, that women should be free to do whatever they want to do and are capable of doing in the church on the same basis as men. A minister can also interpret to such women the importance of the "feminine" side of God from the theological and social standpoint.

Lots of men in the church are open to the issues that women are raising about church life and the reinterpretation of theology. Often they would like some help in understanding just what the changes may mean for the church, and how to implement such changes for the sake of the men as well as the women. Other men are resistant and frightened, however, sometimes because they are worried that women want to "take over" the church, sometimes because they have a vague feeling that it just "isn't right." An enlightened minister or counselor can help interpret to men what women are saying and encourage them to see that the changes sought mean liberation for them as well as for women.

Reshaping Theology

Many women are discovering with surprise and relief that, although the Bible has often been used as the basis for limiting the participation of women in church life, Jesus believed in women as equals. His treatment of women and his remarks about them provide no basis for the subsequent attitude of the church. Women react in different ways to this new awareness! Some say, "So what! It hasn't done us any good. A religion which can lend itself to such excesses as Christianity has experienced in this regard cannot speak with the voice of God." Some of these women are leaving the church altogether.

Theologian Mary Daly is the most articulate representative of those who question whether Christianity can truly speak to women. Her deeply moving and challenging book *Beyond God the Father* is "must" reading for ministers and pastoral

counselors.* Other women believe that since the original in-
tent of the religion founded by Jesus was to include women as
whole persons, the church can be saved. Such women, a
number of them theologians, are struggling to reinterpret the
Christian faith and construct a new theology which will express and affirm the experience of both women and men.

The rising consciousness of women and the development of
a "new theology" have numerous practical consequences for
ongoing church life. What are some of the changes that
women are beginning to insist upon? The following list of
items, developed during a consciousness raising group in a
local church, was presented to the church governing body.
The Women's Task Force asks that our church:

1. Use women in the pulpit from time to time and consider
hiring a woman minister for our staff.

2. Ask the education committee and teachers to review the
church school literature with a view to eliminating whatever
sexism it contains.

3. Use women and girls equally with men and boys as ush-
ers and acolytes.

4. Have women study-leaders and speakers at church meetings.

5. Present "women's issues" like the Equal Rights Amend-
ment and abortion to the congregation for such individual
and corporate action as money raising and letter writing.

6. Buy library books which deal with women in history and
feminist theology.

7. Eliminate sexist and noninclusive language from the liturgy and hymns used in the services, either by using "feminine" as well as "masculine" terms for God or by eliminating
altogether words which refer to sex.

8. Encourage and provide resources for all church groups
—administrative bodies, men's and women's groups, study
groups, church school and youth groups—to study the history
and present status of women in the church and society.

9. Start some study groups specifically on Bible study from

the feminist viewpoint, on feminist theology, and on human liberation.

10. In all church publications, refer to women by their own names (Mary Brown) rather than by their relationship to a man (Mrs. John Brown) or lack of it, and use Ms. instead of Miss or Mrs.

11. Start consciousness raising groups for both women and men.

12. As a consciousness raising experience, conduct a feminist worship service in which all language is female instead of male and all leaders are female.

Among the most striking and potent of the proposed changes is item 7. We are so used to speaking of God as Father, Lord, and King and to the use of the He and Him pronouns, that it is hard to feel comfortable with feminine words and concepts. But women are becoming aware that the language we use and the behavior we condone reinforce each other. So besides feeling left out, some women also realize that the concept of God as male inevitably supports both the lower status of women and a society whose dominant value is power instead of love. It's possible to eliminate the male pronouns and titles and simply refer to God as God. It's also possible to speak of God sometimes as Him and sometimes as Her, and as Mother as well as Father. Since God is androgynous (male-female) or gynandrous (female-male), from a theological point of view either of these solutions is theologically sound. At the same time, such changes serve to remind us of the need for getting the "feminine" back into our concept of God.

A Program for Pastoral Action

Ministers who are truly concerned about sexism in the church can take positive action. There is much that can be done by way of developing a "whole" or androgynous theology and church life. Specifically, pastors can do the following:

1. Use inclusive language in your sermons and elsewhere —humankind instead of mankind, human being instead of man.

2. Use non-sexist jokes and illustrations in your speaking and conversation.

3. Use language that does not refer to women in negative terms (old maid, divorcée, witchy, woman driver).

4. Read and study feminist theology and women's history.*

5. Examine your own theology and the sexist character of the terms you use for God.

6. Become familiar with the many suggestions for eliminating sexism in worship and liturgy.†

7. Examine your own attitude toward equality as a basic human right and an ethical issue for the church.

8. Help your church to implement the twelve suggestions listed above.

Sexism in the Church Schools

Probably the most hopeful area in the long run for bringing about change in the life of the church is that of education. Much of what happens to women (and men too) in the church begins in the nurseries of religious education. The toys we provide, the adult caretakers who relate to children, the pictures and literature we use all have a profound effect on our adult consciousness of what women and men are supposed to be like in the church and outside of it.‡ We can include men as "sitters" in the nursery and as church school teachers in the early years. We can encourage girls and boys to participate in church life according to their interests rather than according to sex.

Church school literature at all levels is inclined to be both obviously and subtly sexist. Church school teachers will note as they begin even a superficial examination of their texts and guides that women and men are nearly always portrayed in stereotypical roles. Girls are pictured watching and being helped, playing with dolls, helping mother. Boys are usually active and inventive. Women are shown wearing aprons, holding babies, wearing nurses' uniforms, typing—rarely if ever as ministers. Men are in professional and work roles, rarely holding babies or doing dishes. Women, except for Ruth and Mary and Martha, are generally left out of Bible study altogether.

Church school teachers are a key group in helping to eliminate sexist attitudes in religious education. It's important that both men and women act as *teachers* and that individually they become aware of their own attitudes about sex roles and identities. They may need to find or create non-sexist materials. That may even mean discontinuing use of the denomination's prescribed literature and letting the publishers know why. Teachers can encourage children in the church school classes to talk about the issues, to examine their own literature and pick out what is accurate or unfair. Even small children looking at pictures can note that daddies care for babies too, while mothers are also professional people and work outside the home. Teachers can be encouraged to become aware of the ways they gear their activities and materials to girls and boys on the basis of sex, like letting the boys do the active things and the girls the quiet ones or grouping the girls in the doll corner and the boys in the construction corner.

Young people's groups provide an important setting for dealing with the issues of sexism in the church. Young people can examine and evaluate their own literature. They can talk about what it means to them to be "masculine" or "feminine" and to what extent they feel those labels limit their lives. They can talk about what they expect and hope for when relating to a person of the other sex—in dating, in marriage, at school, on the job. A sex education course led by a female-male team is an ideal place to examine the stereotypes of "feminine" passiveness and "masculine" aggressiveness. The confirmation class is another setting in which young people can focus on the issues of sexism in the Bible, in theology, and in the church. Prospective young church members need to know about the "feminine" in the Judeo-Christian tradition and about modern feminist theology.

Parents hold the key to attitudes among new generations of children; thus parent education is among the most vital concerns in the church. Parents groups of any kind can examine parental attitudes to sex roles and the implications of those attitudes for the wholeness and happiness of children. Parents can look at how they feel about their own programming as women, as men, as mothers, as fathers, and at whether they are providing their children with a home setting which encourages them to grow as fully as they possibly can without the limitations of sex stereotyping. Literature about child raising for parents can be examined for its sexism. Parents can be involved in the planning of church school curricula and in the assessment of church school literature.

Other Groups in the Church

Consciousness raising about sexism in the church can happen in all church groups. It can provide the theme and focus for staff and committee meetings, women's and men's societies, board meetings, trustees meetings, Bible study groups, prayer groups, marriage enrichment groups, even choir rehearsal. It should obviously loom large in all kinds of individual and group counseling.

Special groups in which consciousness raising is the primary focus are the most direct way of getting at the issues of sexism. Such groups are usually grass roots efforts developing out of the concerns of one or more persons who have become aware of their feelings about women in the church. The twelve recommendations listed above came from such a group after it had met for a series of six sessions. In another church, a consciousness raising group developed into a program series, open to everyone, studying the relationship of the women's movement to the other ethical concerns of the church. Men's groups and mixed groups also are frequently organized around consciousness raising, as people in churches become more aware of the issues. Where there seem not to be any interested individuals, the minister can often stimulate an interest. Specific techniques for organizing and running such consciousness raising groups are suggested in the next chapter.

Theologian Nelle Morton has remarked that "any theology developed by one sex, out of the experiences of one sex, cannot be lived out of as if it were a whole theology."* Women and men both are impoverished by a religious and spiritual life that does not include the full participation of both sexes in every facet of church life. A whole theology, in which the "feminine" and the "masculine" are conjoined, would encourage the development of people who are more whole. And a more whole people is more able and more likely to foster the nurturing of a world in which the abundant life is possible for all.

6. Techniques for Counseling and Consciousness Raising

Healthy growth involves fulfillment, to varying degrees, in all of these dimensions. We all need to be dependent and close at times; we all seek distance, self-sufficiency, and solitude at times; and we all welcome challenge, self-assertion, and even aggression at times. Each human being is a unique and creative blend of endowment, opportunity, and growth.*
—Alexandra Symonds

The emphasis of this book so far has been largely on awarenesses, on attitudes important for counselors and ministers as they face the ethical and psychological issues growing out of the rising consciousness of women. The present chapter suggests some specific techniques that can help people become aware of the boxes they are in and how to get out of them.

Some of the techniques described here are suitable for use with groups or individuals or couples when the main focus is on reeducation or consciousness raising with normally functioning people. Others are more suitable for the counseling situation. Some work well in either setting. With a little imagination, the counselor or minister can adapt any of them to fit particular needs.

Consciousness Raising Groups

Consciousness raising (CR) groups are usually made up of women, at least in the beginning, since it is generally women who are raising the issues. Several women who feel the need can begin such a group. Sometimes the pastor must ferret out these women, who are often silent because they fear ridicule or because they feel alone. In either case a low-key announcement in the church bulletin may attract women who have not felt free to voice their feelings: "A consciousness raising group will begin Monday evening at 7:30 in the lounge. Interested women are invited to attend." Sometimes the very term *consciousness raising* scares some women who would otherwise be interested, in which case the following might be better: "A group of women interested in women's issues as they relate to the church will meet . . . If you are interested come and help us decide how to proceed."

Leadership of a CR group is an important consideration. The first women's CR groups were leaderless since a major goal of the women's movement has been to challenge the hierarchical nature of our social system. But since that system is deeply ingrained, leaderless groups often have trouble getting off the ground. Often someone needs to take the lead in the beginning. Sometimes those women who have initiated the idea will do so, throwing out for discussion whatever issues are of concern to them. If there are no women willing to take the leadership in the beginning, the pastor can appear at the first meeting and simply describe the envisioned purpose of the group and ask for response—are they interested and, if not, what *did* they come to the meeting expecting and hoping for? If the pastor is a man he should make it clear that he is merely taking the initiative in getting the group started and that he will not be present after the first meeting—or maybe even through all of that—since it can't be a CR group for women if a man is present. If the pastor is a woman then of course she can take the leadership of the group as long as leadership is needed. The goal of the leader should always be to lose her job, that is, to become as soon as possible simply a temporary facilitator and group member. Since she is also a woman with personal experience of the "feminine," it's easy for that to happen. Soon the facilitating can become a rotating function among the members of the group.* CR groups are most successful when all members are interested in change, both personal and social.

Men's CR groups usually begin in response to the change in women. Sometimes such a group is made up of the husbands of women in a women's CR group. Or sometimes the members are men who are feeling the pain of changes in their own lives which have resulted from the changes in women. Of course there's no reason that such a group couldn't grow from men's own awareness of need for change in their consciousness independent of women. Considerations for beginning and leading a men's group would be the same as those for women. The leader should always be a man, who should become a facilitator as quickly as possible and then share that function with other members of the group. Since he is a man, with personal experience of the male box, he can do that if he is willing to share his own feelings and experience.

Mixed CR groups sometimes begin as just that, or they sometimes happen when a women's and a men's group decide to get together for an occasional session or a series of sessions. If such a group is an ongoing one it is also a good idea for the women and the men to meet in separate groups from time to time, since women and men, at our present stage of evolution, always behave differently in the presence of the other sex. Mixed CR groups can be for singles or couples or both; they can mix ages or bring together persons of a particular bracket. Every marriage enrichment group, every church school class can and should be a CR group.

The classical technique for a consciousness raising group is simple. Each session begins with a "go around" in which each member of the group says in five minutes or less whatever is on her or his mind in response to a particular topic. The first meeting might focus simply on why each person is there and what he or she expects or hopes for. Anyone can pass. This method provides shy ones with an opportunity to speak up which they might not have, or take, or claim in a free-for-all discussion. It also limits gregarious and garrulous persons. Following the "go-around" the discussion can become less structured, with the facilitator helping merely to keep people on the subject and see that all get a chance to contribute. At the end of the first meeting the participants can decide how they wish to proceed. It is usually wise to set a limit on the number of sessions, anywhere from six to ten, and to limit size of the group to ten people or fewer. If the response to the first call has been enthusiastic, maybe two groups will be formed. Most consciousness raising groups decide each time on a topic for the next meeting and proceed each time with a go-around on that topic. There is a variety of topics suitable for women's groups that can easily be adapted to men's or mixed groups:

How do you feel men see you?

Why did you marry the man you did?

How do you feel about housework?

Do you think what you do with your day is as important as what your husband does with his?

What did (do) you want to do in life?" What kept (keeps) you from doing it?

What does it mean to you to be "feminine"? Do you like it?

What does "masculine" mean to you? Do you like it?

What hopes do you have for your daughter? for your son? Are these hopes different? Why?

Do you feel you are discriminated against by the church?

What was your husband's reaction when you got your consciousness raised?

How do you feel about the male "heart attack syndrome"?

How does it feel to be single in a couple-oriented society?

These topics are suitable for other kinds of groups as well—youth, parent, marriage, premarriage—and in all kinds of counseling and therapy groups. Every group will of course have additional topics of its own to suggest.

Other Consciousness Raising Techniques

I have described the specific approach to consciousness raising evolved within the women's movement. The following techniques are suitable not only for CR groups but in other settings as well.

The Fishbowl

The fishbowl technique illustrated at the beginning of chapter 1 is one of the most dramatically successful methods for providing women and men in groups large or small with the opportunity for deepening their understanding of people of both sexes. It can of course be used to deal with any issue. When the issue is female-male relationships, then it is important that the first group in the center circle be women, since it is women who are challenging the traditional relationship between the sexes.

The "fish" in this inner circle can begin in various ways. Sometimes there is a spontaneous beginning because issues have already been raised and the participants can hardly wait to get started. Usually, however, it is wise to have a particular topic like one of those listed above, or like the quotation from the restaurant plaque which Carol read to start the fishbowl in chapter 1. The women begin with a go-around followed by discussion lasting about forty-five minutes. Then the men become the "fish" while the women act as observers.

It is important that the observers be reminded that they may listen but not respond. Their turn will come. When the men are in the fishbowl they can be asked to respond to whatever the women have been saying and/or they may discuss a question such as "How does it feel to be a man in a world where you are always supposed to be strong and competent?"

Following the second go-around and discussion of forty-five minutes the two groups get together in a single circle to talk about what they have been hearing from each other. By this time feelings are running high, and women and men are anxious to talk to each other. The allotted forty-five minutes are likely to seem much too short to deal with all the pain and anger that surfaces and needs expression.

If the fishbowl is a demonstration group, as in connection with a workshop or conference, a fourth step which allows the larger audience to get involved is also important. In such a setting the inner circle groups may need to be smaller and the allotted times shorter.

Whatever the setting, the fishbowl requires plenty of time for debriefing. The people can be encouraged to continue their debriefing with each other even after the experience is over. A fishbowl experience can be leaderless, or it can have a leader who gives direction and keeps the schedule moving but actually participates only when other members of the same sex are involved. Ideal for such an experience is a female-male leadership team.

The fishbowl technique can be used in consciousness raising groups, of course. It has also been used to great advantage in singles groups, divorce recovery groups, young people's groups, parents groups, marriage enrichment groups, premarriage groups, marriage counseling groups, therapy groups of women and men, professional conferences, and as a demonstration at any workshop or conference on human liberation.

Role Reversal

Role reversal is another effective technique. It is especially useful for helping people get a feel for what the *other* sex experiences. The experience of one couple in counseling may serve as an example.

Alice and Mike were disagreeing about whether to have another child or not. Mike wanted one and Alice didn't. The counselor, after listening to them argue from their own points of view suggested that they reverse roles and argue for the other side. She asked them first to switch chairs and to close their eyes and imagine themselves in the body and role of the other one. Then after a few moments of silence, she suggested that they open their eyes and talk to each other from their new positions:

MIKE: Well, gee whiz, I just can't stand the thought of that nine months of feeling awful, and being too fat, and never being able to lay it down.

ALICE: Last time you enjoyed it. You said it was an experience you wouldn't want to miss, and you were really excited about having another little life growing inside of you.

MIKE: Yes, but I've done that now, and I know that after the ninth month is over I'll be stuck at home for years with another child. I'm just now getting back into things after being tied down with the last one.

ALICE: You sound like you hated every minute of the whole thing—like there haven't been any good things about it, like we never should have had children in the first place.

MIKE: No, that isn't it. Lots of it has been good and I'm glad we did it. But now I just want to get on to other things. I don't want to start that whole thing over again. It's time for a new phase now. Besides, think of all the fun we can have together when I don't have to be so tied down anymore. I might even go back to work and bring in some extra money.

ALICE: Well, that wouldn't be a bad idea. But I always have wanted a son—to carry on the family name, you know, make me feel like a real man!

MIKE: Sounds like you don't think our daughter is as good as a boy would be! Who cares about the family name, anyway!

It's interesting that in this exchange, what got expressed was not just what each had actually heard from the other at various times, but also what each other thought the other was really feeling. Mike had never said he felt disappointed about not having a son, but Alice suspected he felt that way. Alice had never said she wanted to go back to work, but Mike suspected that she did. The role reversal helped each of them to get in touch with how the other was really feeling. Their interchange also brought out some issues that each had been unwilling to risk discussing openly with the other.

An even more dramatic experience of role reversal can be had by assigning the couple the job of actually reversing roles for a whole week, or at least a few days or a weekend at home. Mike couldn't very well go home and have a baby, but he could spend a weekend taking full charge of the children and the house while Alice went off to study or to hunt a job. That would give each a taste of the other's role.

Judy and Tim both had jobs outside the home. They kept a running battle going for some time about whether Tim should share the chores of housekeeping and child care so that

Judy wouldn't have two full time jobs. For a week they tried an actual role reversal. Tim took charge of the household evenings and weekends and did all the things Judy ordinarily did at home. After that he stopped talking about the housework being "not really that much of a job," and started doing his share of it. Assignments of this sort assume a willingness on the part of both partners not only to understand the feelings and activities of the other but also to work out a lifestyle fair to both.

In a group, role reversal can also be effective if one couple takes the roles of another couple, perhaps again reversing the sexes. Or the sexes can stay the same while one couple acts out another couple's conflict. Judy and Tim can play Mike and Alice or Alice and Mike, and vice versa. With a little imagination *role playing* and *role reversal* can effectively be combined in a variety of ways.

In a consciousness raising group or youth group role reversal by sexes can be a moving and at times a hilarious experience. Asking a man to react—as a woman—to the statement "Woman's place is in the home" can often be funny, as well as a deeply shaking experience for all the people present. On one such occasion a young woman discovered through the role reversal exercise that the youth she was dating was looking forward to marrying a wife who wanted lots of children. That was the beginning of a consciousness raising experience for both of them, as well as for the total group.

The role reversal technique can prove useful in any of the groups where the fishbowl would also be effective—except in demonstration settings. It is particularly effective in conjoint and group marriage and premarriage counseling.

Fantasy

Fantasy of any kind can be a powerful way to get in touch with whatever is going on inside a person. It can be highly effective in helping people get in touch with their inner feelings about being boxed in and with the ways in which they stereotype the other sex. In any kind of counseling and con-

sciousness raising it is well to begin with relatively nonthreat-
ening fantasies such as the "Box and Meadow" before moving
into the fantasies detailed below.*

Fantasies are done with eyes closed so that people can more
easily get inside themselves. Every fantasy begins with asking
the participants to get in touch with their bodies as follows
(each ellipsis signifies a pause, the length of which remains at
the discretion of the leader).

Body Awareness. Close your eyes . . . be aware of your
body . . . notice any areas that are uncomfortable or tense . . .
squirm around if you need to get more comfortable . . . take
off your shoes if you like . . . now just be aware of your body
again. . . . Now tighten up all your muscles from your toes to
your scalp, every muscle, knees, fingers, cheeks, toes, neck,
everything; hold it a minute—and let go . . . do that again. . . .
Now, become aware of your breathing . . . feel the air going
in and out . . . follow the air as it flows. . . . Now take some
shallow panting breaths . . . now breathe as deeply as you can
. . . notice how different those two ways of breathing feel . . .
now let your breathing go wherever it's comfortable and re-
laxed for you . . . (Then the leader can move immediately into
the fantasy).

Sex Reversal Fantasy. With your eyes still closed become
aware again of your body . . . how do you feel about your
body? . . . what parts do you like? . . . what parts don't you
like? . . . be aware of your feelings about your body in this
moment. . . . Now, with your eyes still closed, see yourself in
your bedroom at night . . . going through your usual routine
of getting ready for bed . . . now you're actually getting into
bed . . . it's dark . . . you're growing drowsy . . . you fall asleep
. . . the night passes . . . morning is coming . . . as you begin to
wake you become aware that there is something different
about you this morning . . . as you come fully awake you are
aware that you are still you, but you have the body of the
other sex. If you're a woman you now have a man's body; if
you're a man you now have a woman's body. . . . Be aware
of how you feel about your new body . . . now get up out of

bed and go over to the mirror . . . look at yourself without any clothes on . . . what are your feelings about your new body? . . . Now go about your usual morning routine for starting your day . . . get dressed . . . do whatever else you usually do. . . . Now I'll allow you sixty seconds to take yourself through a typical day in your life . . . you're still you . . . you'll do your usual things . . . but in the body of the other sex. . . . As you go through your day notice how you feel in your new body . . . how you behave . . . how people respond to you . . . be aware of all your feelings as you go about a typical day in your life . . . (the leader waits at this point for about sixty seconds). . . . Now, begin to bring your day to a close . . . you're back again in your bedroom at night . . . getting ready for bed . . . going to bed . . . it's dark . . . you're growing drowsy . . . you fall asleep . . . the night passes . . . morning is coming . . . you're waking up . . . and as you wake you find you have your own body back again. . . . Be aware of your feelings about having your own body back. . . . Now, come back to this room where we are meeting and open your eyes. . . .

After the fantasy, the procedure calls for everyone to turn to another person and for these two partners to share with one another (in about five minutes) what the fantasy experience was like for them. Then in the group as a whole the leader asks first the men to suggest words that describe how they felt when they were in the body of the other sex; these words are listed on the chalkboard in a column. After that the women are asked to suggest words that describe their feelings in the body of a man, and these words are listed in another column. The columns usually look something like this:

How Men Feel in a Woman's Body	*How Women Feel in a Man's Body*
vulnerable	strength
embarrassed	strange
frightened	unhappy
out of place	awkward
excitement	powerful
curiosity	barren

How Men Feel in a Woman's Body	*How Women Feel in a Man's Body*
normal	freedom
disgust	delight
dependent	taken seriously
cautious	responsible
wow!	muscular
object	respected
childlike	thrustful
fun	newness
unreal	exhilaration
neat	easier
like a breast	not me

Participants are then asked what general impressions they get from the two lists of words. Of course it is usually quite clear to everyone that the words men use to describe their feelings about being a woman tend to be weak or negative or sexual words, while women use more strong and positive words to describe their experience in a male body. The experience confronts people with the way they themselves tend to label the sexes, even though intellectually they may say they "don't feel that way."

This fantasy also provides the opportunity for people to become aware of how androgynous (or gynandrous) they are. To what extent do I affirm and integrate my "feminine" side (if I am a man) or my "masculine" side (if I am a woman)?

The sex reversal fantasy can be used in any setting where the issue is consciousness raising or sex stereotyping or wholeness. It's an excellent "kick-off" exercise for groups large or small. In a large group it's important that the first sharing of the experience with an individual partner be allotted adequate time and that in the larger discussion those who wish be given plenty of opportunity to express their reactions. When the fantasy is used with a couple in counseling the two kinds of debriefing are done together with the counselor. Although the fantasy experience can be anxiety producing for some people, those who are too deeply threatened by it will "turn it off" at the fantasy stage. They will be "unable" to put themselves into the body of the other sex. People who in the debriefing mention having had that problem can be encouraged to look at what that "inability" says to them, without any suggestion or accusation that they were really afraid. It is, in fact, usually the strongly "feminine" and strongly "masculine" persons who have difficulty with the sex reversal fantasy.

Woman Domination Fantasy. Another useful consciousness raising fantasy is the woman domination fantasy. It helps women to get in touch with their own power needs, and men to feel what it is like to be one down. The fantasy is too long to describe here, but it is easily available elsewhere and can be adapted by the imaginative leader.* It consists of asking people to imagine themselves in a culture where nearly all the people in charge, from the President to the sanitation worker, are women, where all the "mothers" are men, and where the male body is seen as weak and unclean. The fantasy is suitable for larger groups of any kind but less effective for a small group or for a counseling setting.

Fantasy of the Unlived Life. The fantasy of the unlived life also helps people to get in touch with their feelings about their own and the other sex. (It too begins with the body awareness exercise.)

Now, with your eyes still closed, imagine yourself born a member of the other sex . . . if you're a woman imagine yourself born a boy baby . . . if you're a man imagine yourself born a girl baby. . . . Imagine yourself now as an infant member of the other sex. . . . Imagine yourself being fed and cuddled and played with by your parents . . . what are they saying to their baby? . . . what are they saying to each other about you? . . . what are their plans for you? . . . Now you are growing older . . . you're a schoolchild, still of the other sex . . . how do you feel as that child . . . what do you like to do? . . . what are your plans . . . who are your friends? . . . Now imagine that you are an adolescent, still of the other sex . . . how do you feel . . . what do you do . . . how do people treat you . . . what are your plans? . . . Now will you take sixty seconds to bring yourself to your present age, still a member of the other sex . . . notice what you do differently than you did in real life . . . notice how you feel about it all. . . . (The leader waits at this point for about sixty seconds.) . . . Now put yourself back into your own body . . . be aware of how that feels . . . be aware of what you're feeling right now. . . . Now, come back to this room where we are meeting and open your eyes . . .

The fantasy of the unlived life must be adapted to the age or age ranges of a particular group. It is especially good in counseling sessions with individuals and couples. Many women experience for the first time an awareness that their parents really wanted a boy. The opposite sometimes happens to men, but more often men become aware of how much of their lives they have spent trying to "get somewhere" instead of enjoying life. All fantasies should be thoroughly debriefed. When they are used in a counseling setting there is usually no problem about that. In a group setting it is essential that people be asked to share their experiences, first as partners, then in the total group; those who still feel stirred up or anxious or angry should be encouraged to talk with someone about it afterwards.

Androgyny Test

Another useful consciousness raising and self awareness device is the Androgyny Test.* It asks the participants to score themselves on a large number of traits generally thought of in our culture as being "feminine" or "masculine" or "neuter." The result determines to what extent a person is considered to be "strongly feminine," "strongly masculine," or "androgynous," somewhat along the lines of the attitudinal study mentioned at the beginning of chapter 2.

Used in a group the Androgyny Test makes an excellent discussion starter on the issues of equality, sex-role stereotyping, and individual wholeness. In a counseling relationship it can help to clarify what is going on between two people. In the counseling situation it is good to have the partners score the test for themselves and then for each other in order to see how their own perceptions of themselves differ from those of their partner.

Picture Gallery

Picture Gallery is also an excellent counseling and/or consciousness raising technique. The leader displays a collection of pictures of all kinds cut from magazines. Pictures of people, landscapes, activities, of machines—any pictures will do. There should be enough pictures so that each person may pick several. The pictures are displayed everywhere about the room.

The participants are asked to wander about the room and choose several pictures which put them in touch with their feelings about themselves as a woman (or as a man) or their feelings about women (or men) in general. In a mixed group, any combination of these assignments would work; the women might be asked to choose pictures that speak to them about women, or the men could choose pictures which make them think about their male experience.

Then the participants are asked to take their several pictures into a previously arranged small group of six or seven persons—or fewer depending on the allotted time—and, using the go-around technique, share with each other what the pictures mean to them. It is remarkable to discover how deeply people can get into their feelings and experiences just by looking at pictures.

Picture Gallery can be used in a counseling setting with only one or two people; or it can be used in a group of any size. It is a helpful technique for letting people get in touch with their feelings about marriage, or about race, as well as about sex stereotypes.

Projective Techniques

The projective techniques of writing and painting are also effective methods both for individual and group use in becoming aware of feelings—and perhaps changing feelings—about sexuality and stereotypical roles. Asking people to draw or to write their feelings about a given subject or person or experience often brings to awareness material which was previously hidden. In a group experience, paper and crayons can be provided and people asked to draw their feelings about women or men. Couples can be asked to draw their marriage.

People can be asked to make a collage from magazine pictures and/or words, or even a sculpture. Make a collage of yourself, of a man, of a woman. Together make a collage of your marriage. In every instance people are then asked to share their drawing or sculpture or collage with another person and/or with the group.

The writing of prose or poetry is also effective. Write the story of your life, of your marriage. Write a make-believe story in which all your dreams come true. Write a poem about yourself. Write a poem to your spouse. Write down something that describes "What is a woman?"—or "What is a man?" Write a fairy tale. Again share what you have written with another person or with a small group.

In all these instances it should be emphasized that what is important is not the finished product but what creating it does to help one become aware of oneself in new ways. The purpose is not to discover hidden artistic talent but to uncover attitudes and feelings about self and others.

Physical Techniques

Along this same line it is a good idea to encourage people to use physical means both to get in touch with and to express the anger that inevitably arises as women and men try to learn to deal with each other differently. Indian wrestling, foam rubber bats,* shouting yes and no at each other at close range and from opposite sides of the room all provide effective, harmless, and fun ways of draining off strong feeling so that talking becomes possible. There are several excellent resources for those interested in using such techniques, all of which can be effective in groups as well as in various kinds of counseling.†

The Intentional Marriage Model

The Intentional Marriage (or Relationship) Model is an extremely useful technique for couples already in an ongoing relationship or perhaps contemplating one. It can help them to assess their feelings about each other and about their relationship, to communicate their needs and expectations to each other, and to contract for ways in which these needs can be met. Described elsewhere in this series, the method is particularly effective as a consciousness raising technique—for making the "unconscious contract" conscious or intentional.* It should always be used as a technique for revising the contract rather than for reinforcing the status quo, even if both partners are satisfied with the latter. It is oppressive if it merely helps people stay in their boxes.

Assertion Training

A behavior change method which is becoming increasingly popular with women as they begin to change their self-image, but which is also appropriate for men who have not adopted the culturally approved "masculine" qualities, is that of Assertion Training.† Users of the method distinguish between "assertion" and "aggression." Assertive behavior is defined as an honest and appropriate expression of feelings in which a person asserts her or his own rights in ways that do not violate the rights of others.

The technique trains people in a series of graduated steps, each requiring more assertiveness than the one before, to speak up or to do things for themselves even at the risk of disapproval from others. Since women very often feel guilty when they begin to assert themselves and to make demands in their own behalf, some opportunity to deal with such guilt feelings is appropriate. In a consciousness raising group women find that they share the experience of guilt with many other women and that guilt too functions to keep women dependent and submissive. This awareness in itself helps to resolve the guilt feelings.

Assertive training needs to be carefully done so that success can be assured at each step before people move on to the next one. A typical beginning assignment for a woman might be the task of doing at a given time something she really wants to do instead of what is routinely expected of her or even what she normally expects of herself at that moment. The contract could be to spend the afternoon reading a book instead of doing the laundry. A second step might be to ask *her* to make the decision next time about where the couple would go out to dinner, even at the risk of incurring the husband's disapproval. Eventually she may develop the courage to enroll in a class, or go back to school, or take a job, even if her husband isn't entirely enthusiastic.

Of course men can benefit from assertion training too, particularly in relation to other men and to their jobs. Because of our culture's programming of the sexes, men are usually more able than women to be assertive without triggering guilt feelings. On the other hand, men's assertion often becomes aggression, in the language of this particular technique, and thus violates the rights of women. Assertion training may help men assert their rights without being aggressive, and women assert theirs without being manipulative.

Study Groups

From the consciousness raising point of view, *study groups* are among the most important means of getting at the issues raised by the changing identities of women and men. Study groups often grow out of consciousness raising groups. Study can become part of the agenda for existing groups in the church, or the focus of independent programs. Ministers and counselors can read and encourage women to read feminist literature, to explore the women's movement, and to organize their own groups for further reading and discussion.

Many of the resources listed in the Bibliography would provide excellent study material for consciousness raising and subsequent action. A study group does not necessarily need a leader; a group of interested people can read and review a number of books, or one book can be read and discussed chapter by chapter, the members taking turns as leader.

Dealing With Anger

It is almost inevitable for anger to result when traditional ways are challenged. Women feel angry when they discover they've been boxed in for a large part of their lifetimes. Some women feel angry when they think they're being pushed to give up old ways. Men get angry when they feel women threatening their positions of superiority and power. Some men get angry when they discover they too are boxed in. What do we do with all that anger?

Often our impulse is to repress it or pretend it isn't there, or to refuse to face the issues that rouse anger. But it is important for ministers and counselors to become aware of their own anger and their ways of handling it, to encourage others to recognize their anger, to talk about it, and to find physical ways of expressing it which are not harmful to other people. It is especially important for women who are becoming aware of their anger to seek out opportunities to be with other women of like mind, because being together helps them to deal with the anger and to find ways of implementing it in creative channels. One purpose of this chapter has been to provide tools and techniques for helping people to become aware of and deal constructively with their anger—not so that it will go away, but so that it can be used to bring about constructive changes in a dehumanizing society.

It isn't possible here to review all the available techniques for consciousness raising or all possible applications of them. Other suggestions are available from many sources, particularly the Task Force on Consciousness Raising of the National Organization for Women and from Women Committed to Women.* The imaginative minister and counselor will find many ways to use and adapt those presented here, and in the process develop new ones to fit particular people and local situations. Counseling and consciousness raising are of course not ends in themselves. Out of them, if they are effective, comes action which will pass along to others the growth that has taken place.

Epilogue: The Cup of the New Relationship

> One can only speculate on what celebration could be were mutuality (love) possible in the community of faith; were the oppressed of the earth trusted to become a valid part of that community.*
> —Nelle Morton

In the earthquake of changing relationships between the sexes it often seems as though the destruction is so great and the landscape so drastically changed that we will never be able to rebuild. When one sex is pushing and the other is resisting, conflict is inevitable. But good counseling theory affirms the fact that conflict can also be creative and growth producing. The growing edge of relationships individually and collectively is the place where there is dissatisfaction and a struggle for change. Anger doesn't mean that we don't want a relationship; it means we want a better one.

Beyond the anger—if we can keep on talking to each other long enough—awaits a relationship between the sexes which can provide the basis for a benevolent society and fullness (wholeness) of life for everyone. Social activists and counselors in many disciplines have long concerned themselves with the relation—or lack of it—between personal growth and social change. How can the focus of the counseling professions on personal fulfillment be justified in view of the great and urgent human concerns about poverty, famine, racism, war, and disease? In the revolution of rising consciousness in women—and therefore in men—personal growth and social change are inseparable. Social change as a result of personal growth toward wholeness is inevitable and far-reaching.

The relationship between the two shows in a number of

obvious ways as well as in subtle ones. For one thing, as women begin to feel strong and to see that they have far more potential than they have ever imagined, they are less apt to land in mental hospitals. For another, the best way to double human brain power without increasing the population is to free women to develop and use their minds. An even more obvious connection between personal growth and social change is that involving the population explosion and the status of women. The United Nations Educational, Scientific, and Cultural Organization points out that the most effective contraceptive is the education of women. UNESCO statistics show that as the status of women rises in a given country the birth rate declines.

More subtle but nonetheless powerful social change also occurs as women and men begin to define themselves differently. As women learn to value their "strong" side, and men their "gentle" side, a change in the collective consciousness and sense of values takes place which leads to a new balancing of the traits previously labeled "feminine" and "masculine." The valuing of women and the valuing of the attributes now so sorely needed to save humankind are inevitably intertwined. Anne McGrew Bennett remarks that our society gives a superior place to men and to the "so-called masculine attributes—physical force, military power, pride of place, exploitation of the earth, dominance over others. So long as our understanding of the nature of God and the nature of personhood lack wholeness we will continue to destroy ourselves and others."*

As we begin to value women and the "feminine" attributes (love, compassion, caring, service, nurturance) equally with men and the "masculine" attributes (strength, courage, power, assertiveness) we may begin to achieve the wholeness which is our only salvation. A balance of these human traits in women and men, in individuals and in society collectively, is an inevitable result of the rising consciousness of women—and therefore of men. The importance of such wholeness is illustrated by our ecological concerns; what we require is a "masculine" instrumentality and a "feminine" nurturing which together will make it possible for us both to use and to preserve our natural resources.

Such a philosophy is inevitably idealistic. It challenges the hierarchical nature not only of our social system but also of our religion. We need a God in whom the polarities of feminine-masculine, good-evil, infinite-finite are united; a God who calls us to continuing discovery of all our potentialities as individuals and as humankind; a God who does not box us in or limit us with arbitrary definitions of what is human; a God we do not "bump into" when we spread our wings or stretch our muscles toward wholeness and toward an open future.* To admit that such a view is idealistic is not to say it is impossible. The question is not Can we? but Will we?

For ministers and counselors, all of this means both a concern for the individual parishioner or counselee and a looking beyond to the social change that can result when individuals are freed to use their fullest potential. Many people are still hoping that the church can meet the new challenges dramatized by the rising consciousness of women in search of spiritual rebirth for themselves and for all of human society. A major task of ministers and counselors, then, is to become more alive, more free, more able to use all their powers to enjoy life, and to encourage that kind of growth in others. Do whatever you can to get out of your own boxes—as persons, as minister, as counselor. Do whatever you can to help other people get out of theirs.

Notes

Page

v. *Fischer, Brennenman, and Bennett, p. 7.

vi. *Ibid.

1. *Miller, *Psychoanalysis and Women*, p. 391.

3. *Nelle Morton, "Toward a Whole Theology," (Address delivered at World Council of Churches Task Force on Women). Available from Women Committed to Women.

6. *Mabel Blake Cohen, "Personal Identity and Sexual Identity," in Miller, *Psychoanalysis and Women*, p. 182.

17. *Ibid., p. 175.

17. †Liz Hargrove, Marriage and Family Counselor, in unpublished paper.

17. ‡Inge Broverman, et al., "Sex Role Stereotypes and Clinical Judgments of Mental Health," Journal of Consulting and Clinical Psychology, Vol. 34, (1970).

18. *Chester, *Women and Madness*, pp. 62, 63.

18. †Ibid., 121–22.

20. *Bem, "Sex Role Adaptability."

20. †Ibid.

23. *Eliade, *Two and the One*, pp. 78–124; Plato, "The Symposium," *The Dialogues of Plato*, trans. B. Jowett (New York: Random House, 1920), 1:316–17.

24. *Violette Lindbeck, "A Theological Analysis of Women's Movements," *Reflection* 69 journal of opinion at Yale Divinity School, New Haven, Conn.: 1972:8.

24. †*Progress Bulletin* (Pomona, Calif.), 13 January 1974, p. D1.

24. ‡Ibid.

25. *Ibid. Further statistics on runaway wives were published in *Psycology Today*, May, 1975, p. 42. They indicate that by 1974 there were 147 missing wives for the same number of missing husbands.

27. *Doris Lessing, *The Summer Before the Dark* (New York: Bantam Books, 1973), p. 15.

27. †Joan Solomon, "Menopause, a Rite of Passage," *Ms. Magazine*, December, 1972.

28. *Lessing, p. 17.

30. *For a relatively liberated and humane treatment of this growing concern see Clinton R. Jones, *Homosexuality and Counseling* (Philadelphia: Fortress Press, 1974).

31. *For a good discussion of the nonjudgmental approach see H. Clinebell, *Growth Counseling for Marriage Enrichment*, p. 54.

33. *Sally Wendkos Olds, "Breaking Out of the Male Image," *McCall's*, September, 1974, p. 48.

34. *Cohen, p. 170.

34. †Bernard, *Future of Marriage*, p. 156.

35. *Foam rubber bats available from Bataca Products, Inc., 360 Water St., Hanover, Mass. 02339.

41. *C. Clinebell, *Meet Me in the Middle*.

45. *For an excellent overview of sex in the total relationship see William H. Masters et al., *The Pleasure Bond* (Boston: Little, Brown & Co., 1974).

46. *Bernard, chap. 7.

46. †*Los Angeles Times*, 6 October 1974. The Census Bureau reports according to the Santa Barbara News-Press, 4/2/76. that in 1975, women in the "prime child-bearing age" had a record low number of babies. Also in 1975, divorces exceeded one million for the first time in history. There were only 2.3 marriages, the fewest number since 1969 although the population has increased since then. Young people continue to postpone marriage until they are older. There were in 1975 more single young people than ever before. There was a significant increase in the number of homes with only one parent, and particularly in the number of homes with single mothers. It is clear that marriage and the family are experiencing major change.

47. *Ibid., 7 January 1976.

47. †Bernard, p. 42.

49. *Quoted in Campbell, *Masks of God, Primitive Mythology*, p. 350.

49. †Ibid., pp. 352–53.

51. *Ibid., p. 314.

51. †See Bibliography section on Women's History, Religious and Secular for resources which discuss these questions.

52. *For examples of some innovative feminist liturgies see in the Bibliography Swidler, and S. and T. Neufer Emswiler.

54. *See the Bibliography section on Feminist Theology.

56. *See the Bibliography sections on Women's History and Feminist Theology for resources.

56. †See the Bibliography section on Resources for Eliminating Sexism in Church Language and Liturgy.

56. ‡For a personal account of one young woman's stereotypical nurturing in church and society see Frieda Armstrong, *To Be Free* (Philadelphia: Fortress Press, 1974).

59. *See note for p. 2.

60. *Alexandra Symonds, "The Liberated Woman, Healthy and Neurotic," *American Journal of Psychoanalysis* 34(1974):177–83.

61. *For an excellent section on starting women's CR groups see Rush, pp. 119–26.

68. *For "Box and Meadow" fantasy see H. Clinebell, p. 29.

71. *Theodora Wells, "Woman, Which Includes Man of Course: An Exerience in Awareness." Available from Women Committed to Women.

72. *Test samples, along with a discussion of their rationale and validity, may be obtained from Sandra Bem at Stanford University.

74. *See the note for p. 45.

74. †See George Bach, *The Intimate Enemy* (New York: Avon Books, 1968); Rush; and Phelps and Austin.

75. *See H. Clinebell.

75. †See the Bibliography for resources on Assertion Training.

77. *Write to National Organization for Women Task Force on Consciousness Raising (addresses listed in Bibliography) as well as denominational task forces.

78. *Fischer, Brenneman, and Bennett, p. 127.

79. *Anne McGrew Bennett (lecture, Claremont Methodist Church, Claremont, Calif., April 13, 1974).

80. *Daly, p. 193.

Annotated Bibliography

Women's History, Religious and Secular:

Campbell, Joseph. *The Masks of God: Primitive Mythology.* vol. 1. New York: Viking Press, 1970.
————. *The Masks of God: Occidental Mythology.* vol. 2. New York: Viking Press, 1970.

Basic resources for an understanding of the Mother Goddess and the influence and role of the "feminine" in mythology, psychology, archeology, and history. Its sexist language is mitigated by an obvious respect for woman and the "feminine."

Davis, Elizabeth Gould. *The First Sex.* New York: Penguin Books, 1971. A comprehensive history of woman—mythological, historical, cultural, religious, and secular.

Magalis, Elaine. *Conduct Becoming a Woman.* Cincinnati: United Methodist Church Service Center, 7820 Reading Road (1973). The struggle of women for autonomy in the Methodist church.

Neumann, Erich. *The Great Mother: An Analysis of the Archetype.* Princeton: Princeton University Press, 1963. A superb study of the "feminine" in the myth, art, and history of many cultures and its implications from the Jungian point of view for the wholeness of humankind.

Rosaldo, Michelle, and Lamphere, Louise. *Woman, Culture and Society.* Stanford: University Press, 1974. An anthology of anthropological studies of women in cultures around the world. The chapter by Nancy Tanner on matrifocality is especially relevant.

Feminist Theology:

Daly, Mary. *Beyond God the Father*. Boston: Beacon Press, 1974. A philosophy of feminism and a new theology which challenges the hierarchical Father-Son tradition of Christianity and suggests the hope which lies in a theology "beyond God the Father."

Fischer, Clare Benedicks; Brenneman, Betsy; and Bennett, Anne McGrew. *Women in a Strange Land: Search for a New Image*. Philadelphia: Fortress Press, 1975. An excellent anthology of writings by women who care about Christianity and the church. Both theology and personal growth are included in the variety of essays.

Ruether, Rosemary Radford. *Religion and Sexism*. New York: Simon and Schuster, 1974. "A glimpse of the history of the relationship of patriarchal religion to feminine imagery and to the actual psychic and social self-images of women." The essays in this anthology are uneven in their perceptiveness and impact. Of particular importance is the chapter by Patricia Martin Doyle.

Women and Psychology:

Chesler, Phyllis. *Women and Madness*. New York: Avon Books, 1972. What pushes women into "madness" and the need for psychological help? What happens to them when they get there? A comprehensive study of the psychological climate of the twentieth century from the standpoint of its effect upon women.

Miller, Jean Baker, ed. *Psychoanalysis and Women*. Baltimore: Penguin Books, 1973. An anthology of writings by "feminist" psychologists past and present with an excellent chapter by the editor, "New Issues, New Approaches."

Rush, Anne Kent. *Getting Clear: Body Work for Women*. New York: Random House, 1973. An outstanding book for help in getting to know oneself physically, psychologically, sexually. Awareness exercises and methods for expressing anger are suggested. There are excellent sections on how to start a consciousness raising group and how to choose a therapist.

Russell, Letty M. *The Liberating Word.* National Council of Task Forces on Sexism in the Bible. Designed for use as a resource in churches, colleges, seminaries, study and action groups. It seeks to assist laity, pastors, college and seminary students in relating the changing consciousness of women and men to the ways we interpret the Bible through worship, study, and action.

Strouse, Jean, ed. *Women and Analysis.* New York: Grossman, 1974. Critiques of essays by the "great fathers and mothers" of psychology by contemporary feminists.

The Male Mystique:

Brenton, Myron. *The American Male.* New York: Coward McCann, 1966.

Fasteau, Mark Feigen. *The Male Machine.* New York: McGraw Hill, 1974.

Steinman, Anne, and Fox, David J. *The Male Dilemma.* New York: Aronson, 1974.

All three of these books describe the damage done to men by traditional role stereotyping and the gains for them in a new relationship between the sexes. The third includes an inventory of "masculine" and "feminine" values useful for helping people get in touch with their own sex-role expectations.

Female-Male Relationships:

Bernard, Jessie. *The Future of Marriage.* New York: Bantam Books, 1972. A survey of studies on marital happiness with an assessment of the future of marriage, especially egalitarian marriage.

Clinebell, Charlotte Holt. *Meet Me in the Middle.* New York: Harper and Row, 1973. A personal story of one woman's changing self-concept and a study of the implications of sex equality for marriage, sex, child rearing, work, human survival.

Clinebell, Howard J., Jr. *Growth Counseling for Marriage Enrichment: Pre-Marriage and the Early Years.* Philadelphia: Fortress Press, 1975. Techniques for working with couples, some of which can be adapted to consciousness raising.

Assertiveness Training:

Albert, R., and Emmons, M. *Your Perfect Right.* San Luis Obispo, Calif.: Impact, 1970. The language is sexist; otherwise a helpful manual.

Phelps, Stanlee, and Austin, Nancy. *The Assertive Woman.* San Luis Obispo, Calif.: Impact, 1975. Besides excellent discussion and practical guides on assertiveness training, there are listed here a number of good exercises for getting in touch with and expressing anger and other strong feelings. Lots of good material for consciousness raising as well.

Androgyny:

Bem, Sandra. "Sex Role Adaptability: One Consequence of Psychological Androgyny." Available from her at the Department of Psychology, Stanford University, Stanford, Calif. A study of the behavior of persons according to their "feminine," "masculine," or androgynous behavior, and the implications of such new awarenesses. Includes her Androgyny Tests.

Eliade, Mircea. *The Two and the One.* New York: Harper and Row, 1962. Religious and mythical androgyny from the point of view of a historian of religion.

Heilbrun, Carolyn. *Toward a Recognition of Androgyny.* New York: Alfred Knopf, 1973. Androgyny in myth and literature and its implications for modern society.

Resources for Eliminating Sexism in Church Language and Literature:

Emswiler, Sharon Neufer, and Emswiler, Thomas Neufer. *Women and Worship.* New York: Harper and Row, 1974.

Swidler, Arlene. *Sistercelebrations: Nine Worship Experiences.* Philadelphia: Fortress Press, 1974.

Both of these books make a number of suggestions and supply some actual worship services aimed toward making church language and liturgy more inclusive from the standpoint of women. Unfortunately, neither goes quite far enough in challenging the inherent maleness of "Father" and "Lord" in the Judeo-Christian tradition. Otherwise the practical guidelines are excellent and the descriptions of the feelings of women outstanding.

Various pamphlets and mimeograped materials on non-sexist language and liturgy as well as other aspects of consciousness raising for the church are available from:

> Women Committed to Women
> 817 W. 34th St.
> Los Angeles, Calif. 90007

> National Organization for Women
> Task Force on Women and Religion
> 5 S. Wabash, Suite 1615
> Chicago, Ill. 60603

> United Church of Christ Women's Task Force
> 466 E. Walnut St.
> Pasadena, Calif. 91101

Other major denominational bodies also have women's task forces and may have material available.